2001 UPDATE
ELECTRONIC COMMERCE
A MANAGERIAL PERSPECTIVE

EFRAIM TURBAN ◆ JAE LEE
DAVID KING ◆ H. MICHAEL CHUNG

Pearson Education

Upper Saddle River, New Jersey 07458

Acknowledgment

*The authors acknowledge
Carmen Wong of Hong Kong
for her contribution
in preparing Update 1.*

Acquisitions Editor: Bob Horan
Associate Editor: Lori Cerreto
Manager, Print Production: Christy Mahon
Manufacturer: VonHoffmann Graphics, Inc.

ISBN 0-13-065311-X
10 9 8 7 6 5 4 3 2 1

Contents

Building an Application with Yahoo! Store

Update 1

1.1 How to Set Up a Virtual Store with Yahoo!

Yahoo! Store (http://store.yahoo.com) provided by Yahoo! is one of the most inexpensive storefront services currently available. It is a good choice for small to midsize businesses as users can easily set up their storefronts in a few hours with several predesigned templates provided by Yahoo! Store. The software is free for ten days. Furthermore, a store created with Yahoo! Store will immediately be launched as part of the Yahoo! Shopping site and subscribed to its search engine once the business is ready to open.

The monthly charge for a Yahoo! Store is US$100 for 50 items or less and US$300 for up to 1,000 items. No setup fee is required in either case (prices valid as of December 2000).

1.2 Different Features of Yahoo! Store

Table 1.1 lists the features that Yahoo! Store supported as of December 2000. Each feature will be discussed in greater detail later in this section.

Table 1.1

Features of the Yahoo! Store

Features	Yahoo! Store
Maximum number of products	18,000 in largest site
Own domain name	Available
External product search	Available (on Yahoo! Shopping)
Store products search engine	Available
Database upload	Available
Graphic upload	Available (automatic thumbnails)
Product display flexibility	Available
Soft goods	Available (downloadable feature)
Product options (e.g., size, color)	Available
Web pages	Static
Computation of invoice pricing	Available
Setting products as specials	Available
Quantity pricing	Automatic
Cross-selling	Available
Tax calculation	Auto calculation by state from table. Real-time CGI available.
Computation of shipping charges	Auto calculation from price or weight tables, from UPS calculator, or real-time CGI.
Order tracking by customer and merchant	Available (to store manager only)
Merchant order notification	Available (by e-mail or fax)
Inventory management	Not available (only able to display availability status on site)
Traffic and sales reports	Available (to store manager only)
Merchant credit card account required	Available
Payment gateway	Included
Initial setup costs	Nil
Hosting fees	US$100 per month for up to 50 products;
	US$300 per month for up to 1,000 products. An additional $100/month will be charged for each additional 1,000 products.
Transaction fees	Nil

1.3 Creating Your Own Store

Three prerequisites are needed to start creating an online store with Yahoo! Store.

1. A computer with a Web browser and Internet access
2. A Yahoo! identification number.
   Apply at http://store.yahoo.com (refer to figure 1.1).
3. A merchant account for processing credit card payments.
   Apply through Bank One via Yahoo!. Such an account is only necessary when starting to run the business for real; it is not essential during the stage of creating a store.

Step 1: Log in or register for a Yahoo! account.

To build a site, go to Yahoo! Store home page (http://store.yahoo.com) and log in. If you already have a Yahoo! Store account, type in your identification number and password into the boxes on the left-hand side (see Figure 1.1). If you do not have a Yahoo! account, you may obtain one by clicking on the link "Sign Up Here."

Step 2: (Create a store.) Name your store.

Once you are in, click on the link "Create a Store" (see Figure 1.2) and fill in the name and ID for your store. The ID will act as the site address for your virtual store, so it must be a unique name. For instance, if you choose *hotfashion* as your ID, then your future store address will read as follows: http://store.yahoo.com/hotfashion (see Figure 1.3). You may create more than one Yahoo! Store with the same user ID and password as long as you give a different store ID to each Yahoo! Store you create. The store will be valid for ten days.

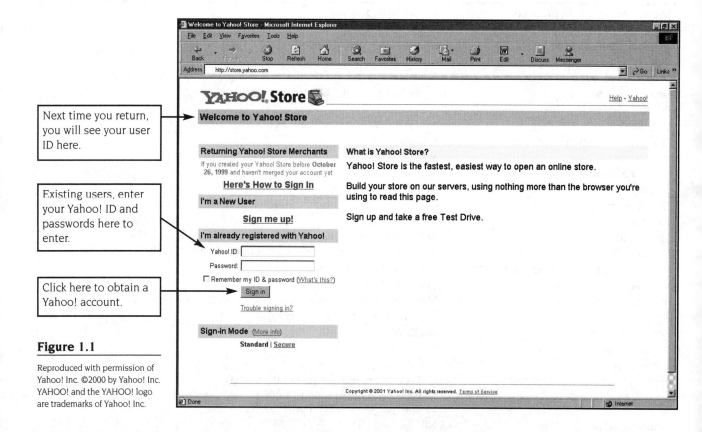

Next time you return, you will see your user ID here.

Existing users, enter your Yahoo! ID and passwords here to enter.

Click here to obtain a Yahoo! account.

Figure 1.1

Reproduced with permission of Yahoo! Inc. ©2000 by Yahoo! Inc. YAHOO! and the YAHOO! logo are trademarks of Yahoo! Inc.

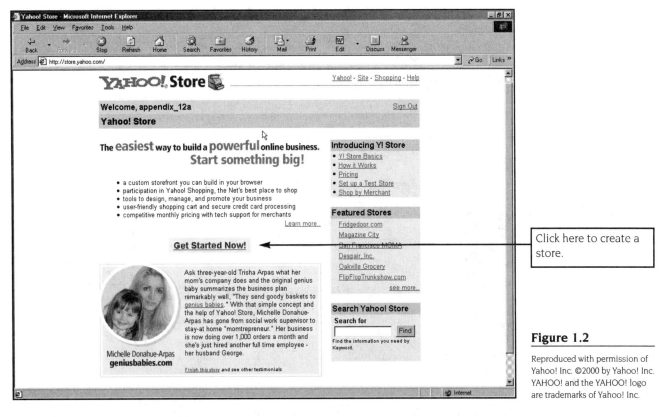

Click here to create a store.

Figure 1.2

Reproduced with permission of Yahoo! Inc. ©2000 by Yahoo! Inc. YAHOO! and the YAHOO! logo are trademarks of Yahoo! Inc.

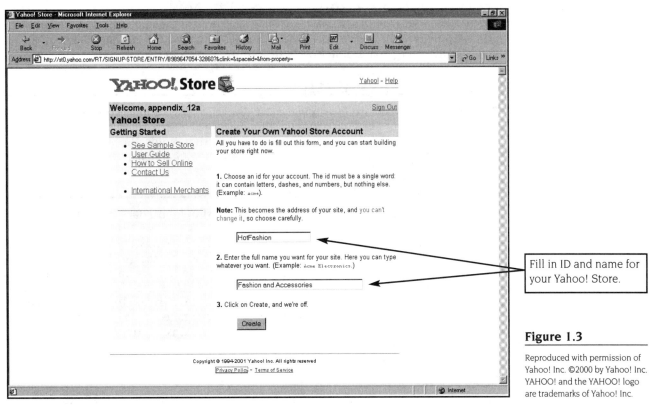

Fill in ID and name for your Yahoo! Store.

Figure 1.3

Reproduced with permission of Yahoo! Inc. ©2000 by Yahoo! Inc. YAHOO! and the YAHOO! logo are trademarks of Yahoo! Inc.

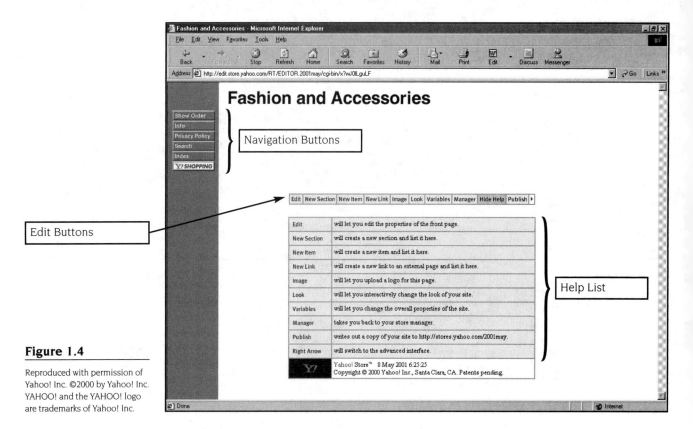

Figure 1.4

Reproduced with permission of Yahoo! Inc. ©2000 by Yahoo! Inc. YAHOO! and the YAHOO! logo are trademarks of Yahoo! Inc.

Step 3: Take a short guided tour.

Next, Yahoo! Store will take you through a short guided tour through the different essential steps to set up the store. The tour will take only a few minutes. Remember, do not click on the Back or Reload buttons during the tour.

1.4   Front-Page Design

Once you get into your store, you will reach the front page and see four items (refer to Figure 1.4). The name of your store will appear in the left-hand corner of the screen. There will also be a button bar on the left side that holds the *navigation buttons*. Additional buttons at the bottom of the screen are the *edit buttons*.

1.5   Sections and Items

There are three different types of pages within the simple interface, namely, *front page*, *section page*, and *item page*.

Items are the individual products available for sale, whereas sections are categories of similar items. For instance, our online store sells clothes and accessories and we want to add a Disney necklace as one of the items. To do this, we first set up a section known as *Accessories* and include several items under it, such as *necklace, bracelet,* and *earrings*. Note that an item page should look different from the section page. On the item page, an enlarged image of the item can be found with some detailed description and an Order button for placing an online order. A section page contains a series of links to different items, and the size of the item image is also diminished.

The Help button will show a list of definitions for the edit buttons.

Step 4: Create a section.

To create a section, click on New Section on the edit button row at the bottom of the front page. You will then see a page containing two fields: Name and Caption.

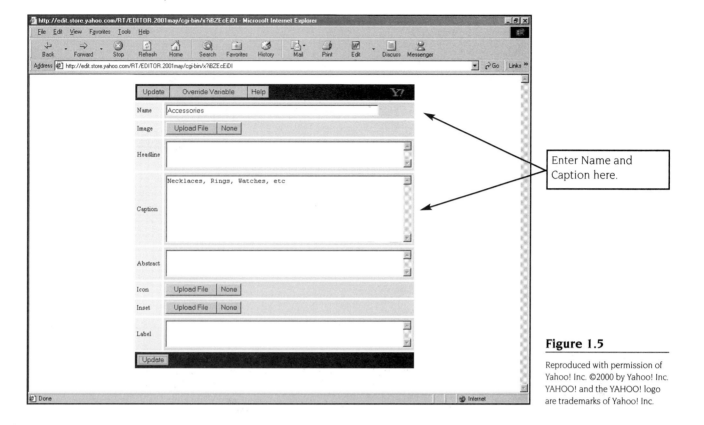

Enter Name and Caption here.

Figure 1.5

Reproduced with permission of Yahoo! Inc. ©2000 by Yahoo! Inc. YAHOO! and the YAHOO! logo are trademarks of Yahoo! Inc.

Enter a name for the section you want to create into the Name field, such as Accessories. Additional descriptions of the section can be entered in the Caption field (see Figure 1.5). These changes can be saved by clicking on the Update button on the top left-hand corner. You will now see your new section named as Accessories directly below the name of the store.

Step 5: Add an item.
Next, we will add an item under this section. Click on New Item and you will see a total of four fields in this page: Name, Code, Price, and Caption. The name of the section, for example, Necklace, is entered into the Name field. The Code field is where you fill in your item's SKU, stock number or ISBN, or any other code to identify the particular product, such as CA123. The selling price is entered in the Price field, such as 200. The dollar sign is optional to fill in, but it is better to state the currency clearly in the Caption field where you can enter descriptive text for the item. Similarly, these changes are saved by clicking on Update. There is no upper limit for the number of items to be included under one section.

Step 6: Upload an image.
A product image or picture can be uploaded onto the store by going to an item page and clicking on the Image button. Such uploading can only be done with Netscape 2.0 or higher versions or Microsoft Internet Explorer 3.0 or higher.

To select the image file to be uploaded, click on the Browse button to locate the file from your local disk drive through the pop-up window. Larger image files require more time. When you find the target file, click on the Send button to upload it to the store. Accordingly, an image can be seen on the related item page (refer to Figure 1.6).

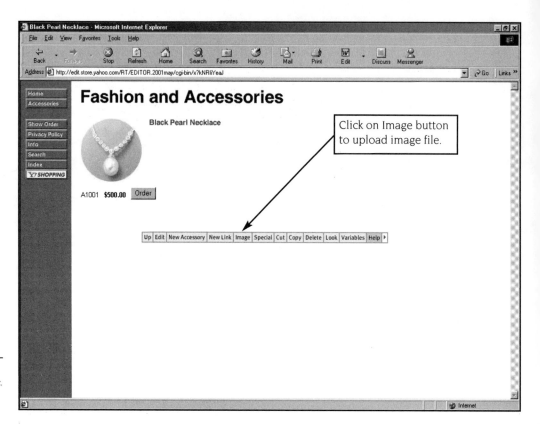

Figure 1.6

Reproduced with permission of Yahoo! Inc. ©2000 by Yahoo! Inc. YAHOO! and the YAHOO! logo are trademarks of Yahoo! Inc.

Step 7: Publish your store.

The most crucial step of setting up an online store is to make it visible to your customers. Such visibility can be achieved by clicking on the Publish button on the front page.

Go to the front page of your Yahoo! Store, and, on the list of edit buttons, click on the last button, the Publish button. It will then change into Published to confirm that the store can be visited via the Internet. The URL for this illustration is **http://store.yahoo.com/hotfashion**.

Step 8: Place a test order.

Orders can be placed by clicking on the Order button on each item page, unless there is a corporate firewall that prevents you from ordering. All items selected would be taken to a shopping cart, which functions similarly to the trolley used in the supermarket. There is no limit on the number of items placed into the shopping cart and you can always pick additional items by clicking on the Keep Shopping button.

When you finish shopping, you may click on Check Out to proceed with filling in the order form. Essential information to input includes shipping and billing addresses, name, and credit card numbers if payment method is set as such. An order number would be assigned to a valid and complete order form that starts from 485 by default.

Step 9: Retrieve an order.

The site manager has several options to retrieve an order. The manager may export the orders to external database software, such as Microsoft Access or Excel, or have Yahoo! fax the orders (but note this feature is only available to companies located in North America). Alternatively, orders can be reviewed on the Internet.

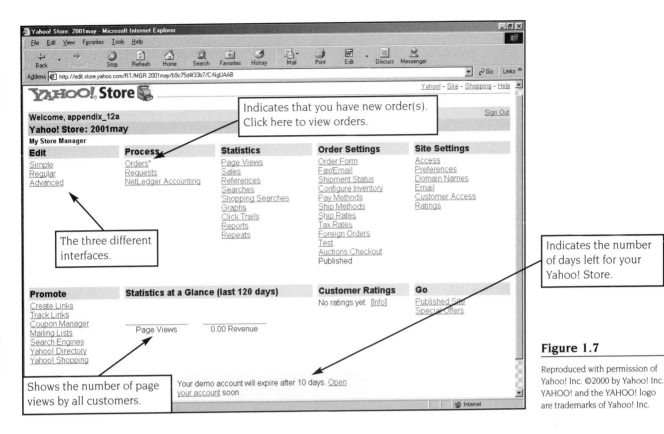

Figure 1.7

Reproduced with permission of Yahoo! Inc. ©2000 by Yahoo! Inc. YAHOO! and the YAHOO! logo are trademarks of Yahoo! Inc.

To view orders online, you must log in as a *store manager* (see Figure 1.7). An editing page would then be displayed with functions and settings that can be modified. By default, Yahoo! Store will automatically put an asterisk next to Order when there are unread orders. Order status can be reviewed by clicking on the Order link.

You may choose to save the order to your hard disk or print a hard copy. Orders received previously will be stored in the server for several months; however, the credit card numbers on the orders should be deleted for security purposes after they have been sitting on Yahoo!'s server for ten days.

Step 10: Add introductory text.

Many stores have an introductory paragraph about the site. Such a paragraph can be added by clicking on the Edit button on the front page. The Message field allows you to enter the details of introduction and multiple paragraphs can be set by separating each of them with blank lines. These changes can be saved by clicking on the Update button.

Step 11: Create a special item.

If you want to draw more attention to some special items, you may put them on the front page so that every visitor to the site can readily see them. This can be done by clicking on the Special button at the bottom of the item page.

Step 11A: Go to the item page and click on the sixth edit button from the left (list the Special button). You will see a thumbnail version of the image (if any), with the name and price of the item (refer to Figure 1.8) on the front page.

Step 11B: To remove the special item, go back to the item page and click on the sixth button on the edit button list (but not the Special button). To keep a flow of repeat customers, change your item on special regularly. Repeat step 11A if you post any other specials for your online store.

Figure 1.8

Reproduced with permission of Yahoo! Inc. ©2000 by Yahoo! Inc. YAHOO! and the YAHOO! logo are trademarks of Yahoo! Inc.

Product on special appearing on the front page of the site in thumbnail image.

Step 12: Edit variables.

The overall properties of your site can be edited by clicking on Variables, an option that is available on every page. Once changes are made under Variables, all pages in the site will be changed accordingly. However, unique properties can be created if you have chosen to override the variables on individual pages.

Step 13: Customize shipping and payment methods.

Payment and shipping methods can be customized by first logging in to the account as a store manager and then clicking on Pay Methods under the Order Setting column. You may select the desired payment method, such as Visa or COD, by clicking Yes next to the method. It is advisable to select COD or Bill Later if you are not in the USA. Other forms of payment can also be specified at the bottom, such as your store charge card. These changes can be saved by clicking on the Update button (Figure 1.9).

Customization of shipping method is also possible by clicking on the type of shipping method preferred and following similar procedures as shown previously.

Step 14: Use the regular and advanced interface.

More features can be added through the regular interface by clicking on Regular under the Edit column. There are more features, fields, and variables in the Regular interface. Clicking on the small red triangle at the end of the edit button row would switch the mode to the Advanced interface where even more buttons can be found. However, the Advanced interface is suitable for experienced programmers only, because all security devices are turned off here. Generally speaking, the Regular interface is adequate for development of an online store.

Step 15: Set discounted prices and quantity pricing.

Discounts can be offered by clicking on Edit on the item page. There are a number of subfields under the Price field. The marked price, for instance, 100, can be

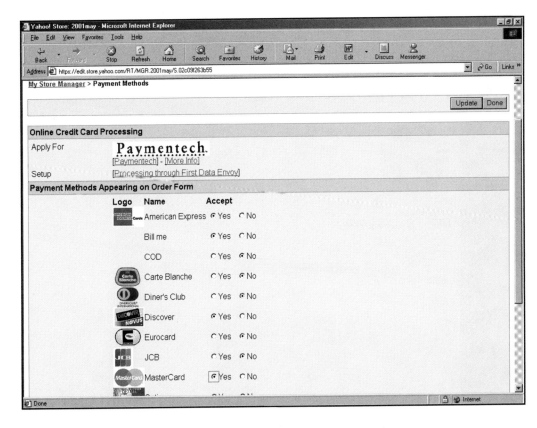

Figure 1.9

Reproduced with permission of
Yahoo! Inc. ©2000 by Yahoo! Inc.
YAHOO! and the YAHOO! logo
are trademarks of Yahoo! Inc.

entered in the Price field while the net price after discounts (say, 80) can be
entered in the Sales Price field. You may save these changes by clicking on the
Update button.

Quantity discounts can also be established by entering the details into the
related field. For example, if a particular item is sold at $10 for one, two for $18,
then 10 for $90, and so forth, the following numbers should be filled in the Price
field:

10   2   18   10   90

Step 16: Determine orderable items.
Stock availability can be shown under the Sales Price field by clicking on Yes (for
available items) or No (for unavailable items) respectively.

Step 17: Set the options feature.
Specification of different colors or sizes can be entered into the Options field. For
instance, different colors, such as black, navy blue, or violet, and different sizes,
such as XS, S, M, and L, can be entered in the following format:

Color: black, navy blue, violet

Size: XS, S, M, L

Each set of options is separated by a blank line and presented as a drop-down
menu on the page where customers may choose the color they want (refer to
Figure 1.10).

Step 17A: Go to the item page, and click on the second button on the edit
button list (Edit). Under the Options column, type in the above format to create
two sets of options. Click on Update to finish.

Figure 1.10

Reproduced with permission of
Yahoo! Inc. ©2000 by Yahoo! Inc.
YAHOO! and the YAHOO! logo
are trademarks of Yahoo! Inc.

Step 18: Add an accessory to an item.

Accessories are additional items at the bottom of an item page. The purpose of adding an accessory is to promote another related item that closely associates with the original item. For example, a tie can be added as an accessory under the item Shirt, instead of starting a new item page for it. An accessory can be added by clicking on the New Accessory button on any item page (refer to Figure 1.11).

Step 19: Cross-sell items.

Cross-selling involves selling related items to a customer when orders are placed. For example, in a fast-food shop, customers are usually asked whether they also want a coke (related item to burger) when they order and purchase a burger.

A "family" has to be defined to facilitate cross-selling. The name of this family can be entered into the Families variables so that the entire set of related items can be edited to assign them to a particular family.

Step 20: Make a store coupon.

Go to the Coupon Manager page in your store manager to create a coupon code. Once you have created the code, send it to your customers via e-mail, or print it on your online store or Web advertising. To redeem the coupon, your customer will only need to input the coupon code on the order form page when checking out. The discount you have specified earlier will be calculated and displayed on the second page of the order form.

Step 21: Keep statistics.

Statistics are also available in the Coupon Manager. This allows you to track the effectiveness of your coupon promotions. You may see how many times each coupon is used, and how much revenue is generated from the specific coupons. This information can help you understand what kind of promotion works best for your online store.

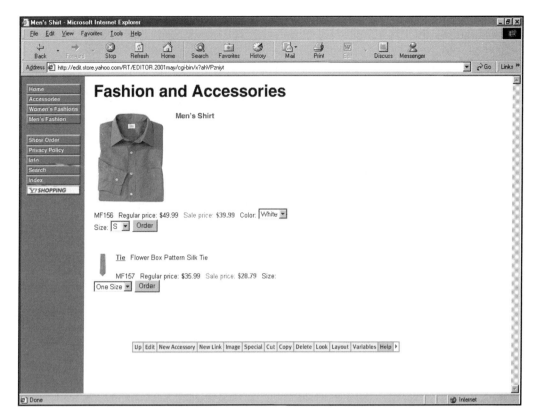

Figure 1.11

Reproduced with permission of Yahoo! Inc. ©2000 by Yahoo! Inc. YAHOO! and the YAHOO! logo are trademarks of Yahoo! Inc.

Step 22: Set shipping and tax rates.

A shipping and tax wizard is available to help set the shipping and tax rates. The shipping rate can be set by clicking on the Ship Rates link under the Order Setting column and then the Auto Setup Wizard link on the top left of the page. Then the base country of the store has to be selected before entering the shipping table and the surcharge for international delivery.

Tax rates can be set by following similar procedures with the Auto Setup Wizard under the Tax Rates link and selecting the appropriate tax rates.

Step 23: Analyze the statistics.

Yahoo! Store offers extensive tracking tools that update statistics once a day. The different tracking tools include the following:

Step 23A: Per Page   The Per Page tool shows the page views and income generated for each page. You will see a thumbnail graph that shows the trend over a particular period on each line. These graphs are useful to ascertain which individual page becomes outdated and no longer attractive to visitors.

Step 23B: Reference   The Reference tool indicates the sites where customers are referred or linked from and how much money they spent on the virtual store.

The actual search keywords entered by visitors and the amount of money they spent using each keyword are available in the Details link under the search engine.

Step 23C: Search   The Search tool shows the search done by visitors. It can highlight the part of the site that draws customer interest, the part that is expected by customers but is missing, and the part that is difficult to locate from the site.

Step 23D: Graphs   The Graphs tool generates graphs of overall trends in the site based on a number of measures such as page views, income and a range of time periods. These graphs are all in .gif format and can be saved to the local disk and imported into applications such as Microsoft Word.

Step 23E: Click Trails Paths taken by individual visitors through the site are shown under the Click Trails tool. It indicates the browsing paths of visitors who have placed items in the shopping cart. Note that the statistics saved under this tool last for sixty days only.

Step 23F: Reports The Reports tool generates a table, which summarizes trends within the site. This report may be exported directly to any database application, such as Microsoft Excel.

Step 23G: Repeat The Repeat tool tracks customers who revisit the site sorted by the number of orders. It matches each order with the name of the customer, the credit card numbers, and the e-mail address.

Step 24: Determine other ways to retrieve orders.

There are alternative ways to retrieve orders apart from those discussed in the previous section. Orders can be sent by fax or e-mail to your real-time application or exported to database applications such as Quickbooks. Advanced users can have their orders sent to their secure Web server in real time.

Step 25: Export Orders to Microsoft Access.

All tables in the site can be downloaded as a tape archive (tar) file. In Unix systems, the tar command can be used to unpack the archive. In Windows, the Win Zip can be employed to do so. The number of files exported is limited to 500.

Step 26: Fax Orders.

Yahoo! Store allows up to two sets of fax numbers to send the orders. This service is free if the receipients are within the United States and Canada.

Orders can be faxed without a cover page to the designated numbers daily (8 A.M.–6 P.M. EST), hourly, or immediately. Each fax has a header such as the following:

Yahoo! Store order hotfashion-675 for HotFashion Company.

Yahoo! Store will try dialing up to fifty times at approximately fifteen-minute intervals in case the receiving fax machine is out of paper or switched off.

Step 27: Print Orders.

Orders can be printed in only two formats: Postscript and PDF. The printing option is available upon retrieval of orders.

Step 28: Perform real-time delivery of orders to your secure Web server.

To have real-time delivery of orders, a URL and a format must be specified. It is advisable to use the Yahoo! format which is a simple CGI script. However, the system also supports the OBI (open buying on the Internet) standard for transferring orders.

The Yahoo! format consists of key-value pairs delivered in HTTP POST request to the specified URL. Example keys are Ship-Name, Card-Number, and Item-Description-1. On the other hand, the OBI/1.1 protocol is documented by the open buying consortium orders, and catalog requests are delivered as "OBI Orders" to the URLs specified.

Step 29: Promote softgoods.

Some storefronts may carry downloadable items for sale on their sites. An example of a downloadable item is software. Yahoo! Store offers the feature that allows a storefront to securely sell downloadable items in its store.

To sell downloadable items, go to the item edit page and upload a file to the Download field specifying a filename for the good to be downloaded.

After ordering a softgood item, the customer can use the Download button on the Order Confirmation page to download the item. Alternatively, the customer can always connect to the Order Status page using the URL from the Order

Confirmation e-mail and start to download the "product." This can also be done from another computer other than the one where the transaction is conducted.

For free downloadable items, simply enter the advanced interface and upload your file to the File pages, then create a link to the file by using either HTML or the New Link button.

Step 30: Make a unique and outstanding site.
There are a few ways to make a site more outstanding and unique than those created with design templates. Ways to achieve this include modifying the navigation buttons (the section buttons) on the left of the page, customizing appearances of buttons, and putting specials as thumbnails.

Step 31: Rearrange the navigation buttons.
By default, the navigation buttons are listed on the left of the page. Their location can be rearranged by switching the pageformat from sidebuttons to, say, topbuttons.

Step 32: Conduct Yahoo! auctions.
Yahoo! auctions is a feature which Yahoo! launched in March 2000 and is free to both buyers and sellers. It allows owners of Yahoo! Stores to participate in the auction platform. Both hot items and hard-to-sell products can be put on sale. This is also a good way to expose different customers to products without extra costs for marketing or new technology.

Step 33: Utilize Yahoo! Auction
Products can be linked directly from the Yahoo! Store to Yahoo! Auction by clicking on the Edit button on an item page. When the auction closes, the winning bidder can click directly into the store to check out and complete the transaction.

Multiple items can also be put on auction by using the Yahoo! Auction Bulk Loader option. And now you can build your own store!

Note that there are several other features available. You can view them, and actually build a store, during the guided tour.

Dynamic Pricing: Auctions and More

Update 2

Learning Objectives

Upon completion of this update, the reader will be able to:

Define the various types of auctions and list their characteristics.

Describe the processes of conducting forward and reverse auctions.

Describe the benefits and limitations of auctions.

Describe the various services that support auctions.

Describe the hazards of e-auction fraud and countermeasures.

Describe bartering and negotiating.

Analyze future directions and the role of m-commerce.

Update Content

2.1   Electronic Auctions in Action: Representative Examples

C2B REVERSE AUCTIONS: DM & S

DM & S is a small trucking company with $1.8 million in annual sales. During 1999, truckers were very busy, but in early 2000 the economy in the United States started to slow down while fuel prices increased. DM & S started to lose money, together with other small movers.

A major problem in trucking is that trucks need to move at certain times, and they may not be full then. Furthermore, on return trips, trucks are usually not completely full. Bert Lampers, owner and CEO of DM & S, had an idea: create a service in which small moving companies bid on jobs of moving individuals. Customers who have flexibility with moving dates can benefit the most. This is basically a **reverse auction** process.

Once customers place their job on **dickerabid.com** (the auction site Bert Lampers created for a cost of $15,000), the truckers can start to bid. For a trucker with a destination and travel date that matches the customers' requirements, hauling anything is better than going with empty space. Simultaneously, customers can get huge discounts while winning truckers can cover at least their fuel expenses. Starting with four truckers and growing to twenty, the site increased DM & S revenue by $14,000 during the first few months of operation. Additional revenue is generated by advertisers that cater to moving people, such as furniture and window blinds companies. The Web site won *Inc.* magazine's third place in Web innovations in 2000.

In this example, DM & S is a third-party auction maker, as well as a buyer (trucker). Larger truckers (movers) have their own Web site, **imove.com**, which provides a considerable amount of information.

Source: Compiled from Inc. Tech, No. 4, 2000, and from dickerabid.com.

B2C AND C2C FORWARD AUCTIONS: DELL COMPUTERS

If you want to buy or sell a used or obsolete Dell product, go to dellauction.com. Whether you are a buyer or a seller, you will find lots of information about the items you are interested in. For example, you can find out if the seller is Dell (B2C) or an individual (C2C), and you will be able to check many product details, such as item warranty and condition (see Figure 2.1). The same goes for general services, such as escrow. Everything is organized for you, from your own personalized shopping cart and account to payments and shipping.

C2C FORWARD AUCTIONS: ALL OF US AT eBAY

A visit to **eBay.com** is a must. EBay is the world's largest auction site with a community of more than 20 million registered users as of spring 2001. The site basically serves individuals, but it caters to small businesses as well. In 2000 it transacted $5 billion in sales, concentrating on collectibles, but other auctions (such as surpluses) were also conducted. In 2001 eBay started to auction fine art in collaboration with **icollector.com** of the United Kingdom. The site also provides for fixed-price trading. EBay operates globally, permitting international trades to take place. Country-specific sites are located in the United States, Canada, France, the United Kingdom, Australia, and Japan. Buyers from more than 150 other countries participate. EBay also offers a business exchange in which small medium enterprises can buy and sell new and used merchandise in B2B or B2C modes.

EBay has 53 local sites in the United States that allow users to easily find items located near them and to browse through items of local interest. In addition, specialty sites, such as eBay Motors, concentrate on specialty items.

Trading can be done from anywhere, anytime. Wireless trading is also possible (see ebay.com). The best way to appreciate eBay is to sell or buy an item in eBay's trading community.

2.2 Fundamentals of Dynamic Pricing and Auctions

The opening vignettes illustrate a variety of dynamic pricing auction mechanisms, which are the topics of this update.

DEFINITION, TYPES, AND CHARACTERISTICS

An **auction** is a market mechanism by which buyers make bids and sellers place offers. Auctions are characterized by the competitive nature by which the final price is reached. A wide variety of online markets qualify as auctions using this definition. Auctions, an established method of commerce for generations, deal with products and services for which conventional marketing channels are ineffective or inefficient. Auctions can expedite the disposal of items that need liquidation or a quick sale. They offer trading opportunities for both buyers and sellers that are not available in the conventional channels, and they ensure prudent execution of contracts.

The Internet provides an infrastructure for executing auctions at lower cost, and with many more involved sellers and buyers. Individual consumers and corporations alike can participate in this rapidly growing and very convenient form of electronic commerce. The Internet auction industry is projected to reach $52 billion in sales by 2002.

850MHz LAPTOP SUPERCOMPUTER: Sexy UltraThin, Carbon Fiber, UltraLite 13.3in Laptop by ACC: the U-2!

Updated: February 2, 2001 11:36:38 AM EST. For up-to-date bidding information on this listing, click on the bid history link.

Listing Type:	**Opening Bid:**
Quick Win	$2,500.00
Time Remaining:	**Quantity:**
6 Days, 23:24:02	1
High Bid:	**Bid Increment:**
$0.00	$250.00
Open Date:	**Listing #:**
1/26/01 12:10 AM EST	33910966
No. of Bids: (History)	
0	
Close Date:	
2/9/01 12:10 AM EST	

Bid Now
Seller Info

Email This Listing to a Friend

Add to Watch List
Shipping/Payment

Selected Features
- 13.3" XGA Active Matrix Color Screen
- Intel Pentium III 850 MHz CPU with 256K cache
- Removable 20G Ultra DMA/33 hard drives
- 64MB SDRAM Expandable to 320MB
- 256KB on-die L2 Cache
- FULL SET OF EXTERNAL PERIPHERALS:
  External 8X DVD-ROM, 24xCDROM, 4X CD-RW, Zip Drive, and?3.5" FDD can be connected externally to the notebook or installed in the Ultra Base
- ULTRA BASE can be used to hold the peripherals, which mount internally or can be used externally through the U-2.
- Internal 56K Data/Fax Modem with 10/100BT Ethernet combo card
- 3D Surround Sound w/ Stereo Speakers & Microphone
- 8MB AGP 3D Graphics
- Long Lasting Intelligent Lithium Ion Battery
- Executive Carrying case
- Ultra Light weight (less than 4 lbs) made of space age carbon fiber plastic is virtually unbreakable.?Much safer than Titanium. Ultra Thin (less than 1")

Ports
- USB
- Fast InfraRed
- 1 Serial, 1 Parallel
- PS/2 KB/Mouse
- Mic-in and Headphone-out
- RJ-11 56K Modem connector
- RJ-45 10/100BT Ethernet connector
- External XGA Video
- 1 Type II or Type III PCMCIA (Card Bus & Zoom Video)
- External drive connector
- Ultra Base docking connector

Software
- Choice of Windows 98 SE or Windows Millennium (Windows 2000 optional)
- Panda AntiVirus Software Office Bundle

Seller Information

Seller Username	COMPAMERICA **(0)**	View Comments on this Seller
Seller Type	Private Party	View All Listings from this seller
		Email Seller
Seller Location	Cranford, NJ, US	

Figure 2.1

A Dell product in an auction

There are several types of auctions, each with its motives and procedures. Klein (1997) classified them into four major categories as shown in Table 2.1. These can be done online or offline.

Traditional Auctions

Traditional auctions, regardless of their type, have several limitations. For example, they generally last only a few minutes, or even seconds, for each item sold. This rapid process may give potential buyers little time to make a decision, so they decide not to bid; therefore, sellers may not get the highest possible price, and bidders may not get what they really want or they pay too much. Also, in many cases, the bidders do not have much time to examine the goods. Since bidders must usually be physically present at auctions, many potential bidders are excluded. Similarly, it may be complicated for sellers to move goods to the auction. Commissions are fairly high, since a place needs to be rented, the auction needs to be advertised, and an auctioneer and other employees need to be paid. Electronic auctioning removes these deficiencies.

Electronic Auctions

Electronic auctions **(e-auctions)** have been in existence for several years on local area networks (see Section 2.6), and were started on the Internet in 1995. They are similar to offline auctions, except that they are done on a computer. Host sites on the Internet act like brokers, offering services for sellers to post their goods for sale and allowing buyers to bid on those items. Many sites have certain etiquette rules that must be adhered to in order to conduct fair business (see eBay.com and Haggle Online, haggle.com). The usaweb.com site provides an Internet auction list and a search engine. Bidfind.com is an auction aggregator that enters hundreds of auction sites and lets you know which items are auctioned at which sites.

Major online auctions offer consumer products, electronic parts, artwork, vacation packages, airline tickets, and collectibles, as well as excess supplies and inventories being auctioned off by B2B markets. Another type of online auction is increasingly used to trade new types of commodities, such as electricity transmission capacities, gas and energy options, and spectrum auctions. Furthermore, conventional business practices that traditionally have relied on contracts and fixed prices are increasingly being converted into auctions with bidding for online procurements.

Table 2.1

Motives of the Participants in Different Auction Types

Auction Type	Coordination mechanism	Price discovery	Allocation mechanism	Distribution mechanism
Buyer role	Short-term acquisition of resources, e.g., for demand peaks, auction as a mechanism to achieve an equilibrium	Often experts/ professional collectors trying to acquire rare items at a reasonable price	Bargain hunting, gambling motive	Bargain hunting, gambling motive; possible side motive: charity
Supplier role	Short-term allocation of resources, load balance	Exposing items for sale to a sufficient breadth of demand, hope for a high price	Clearance of inventory	Attention, direct sales channel, public relations; possible side motive: charity
Auctioneer/ Intermediary role	Often electronic auction without auctioneer	Achieve high breadth and depth of the auctions, high trading volume results in high returns, competitive advantage over other auctions	Achieve high breadth and depth of the auctions, high trading volume results in high returns, competitive advantage over other auctions	Limited role because of supplier-buyer relation; possible function as service provider for the supplier side

Source: Klein (1997), p. 4. Used by permission.

Although it is true that the majority of consumer goods—except those just discussed—are not suitable for auctions, and that for these items conventional selling—such as posted price retailing—will be more than adequate, the flexibility offered by online auction trading may offer innovative market processes. For example, instead of searching for products and vendors by visiting sellers' Web sites, a buyer may solicit offers from all potential sellers. Such a buying mechanism is so innovative that it has the potential to be used in almost all types of consumer goods, as will be shown later when the concept of "name-your-own-price" is discussed.

Figure 2.2

Types of Dynamic Pricing

DYNAMIC PRICING AND TYPES OF AUCTIONS

The major characteristic of an auction is that it is based on dynamic pricing.

Dynamic Pricing refers to a commerce transaction in which prices are not fixed. In contrast, catalog prices are fixed and so are prices in department stores, supermarkets, and many storefronts.

Dynamic pricing appears in several forms. Perhaps the oldest one is *negotiation and bargaining*, which has been practiced for many generations in open-air markets. It is customary to classify dynamic pricing into four major categories depending on how many buyers and sellers are involved, as shown in Figure 2.2.

As can be seen in Figure 2.2, four possible configurations exist:

1. **One buyer, one seller.** In this case one can use negotiation, bargaining, or bartering. The resulting price will be determined by bargaining power, supply and demand in the item's market, and possibly business environment factors.
2. **One seller, many potential buyers.** In this case the seller uses forward auctions, or just auctions. There are four major types of forward auctions: **English auction, Yankee auction, Dutch auction,** and **Free-Fall auction**.

English Auctions

Buyers bid sequentially on one item at a time. A minimum bid that specifies the smallest amount that can be entered is usually part of an English auction. The auction will continue until no more bids are rendered, or until the auction time is over. The winner is the one with the highest bid, if price is the only criteria. If other criteria—such as payment arrangement or how quickly the buyer can take the item—are considered, the winner is selected from those who submitted high bids. Forward auctions can take days on the Internet, but online auctions can be in real time (live) and may take only minutes. English auctions are used in C2C, B2C, B2B, and G2B markets. The process is shown in Figure 2.3.

Yankee Auctions

A seller offers multiple identical items usually with a minimum bid. Bidders can bid for any amount above the minimum. A winner pays the exact price of his winning bid (the highest bid). The auction can be reverse auction too.

Dutch Auctions

Prices start at a very high level, as has been done for many decades in the international flowers market in the Netherlands. The price is slowly reduced and the bidders specify the quantity they want to buy at the declining price. Dutch auctions are designed for multiple identical items. Before the Internet, the process in the Netherlands was done manually using a big clock whose hands showed the price. Now the clock is computerized (see Figure 2.4). Once a bidder is willing to pay the price indicated by the auctioneer, the quantity available is adjusted until the entire quantity is sold. Dutch auctions happen very fast, even when conducted on the Internet. In contrast, English auctions may take days. There are variations of this method.

The following describes how a Dutch auction is conducted at eBay:

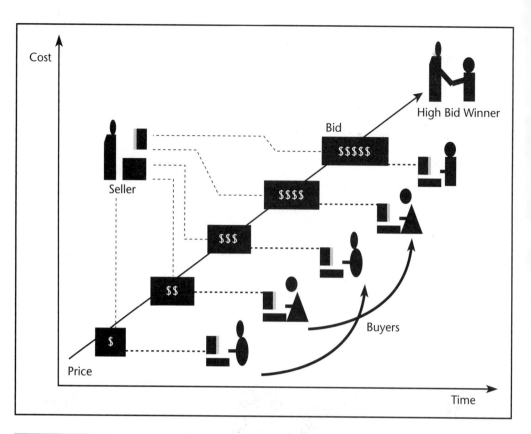

Figure 2.3

English auction, ascending price

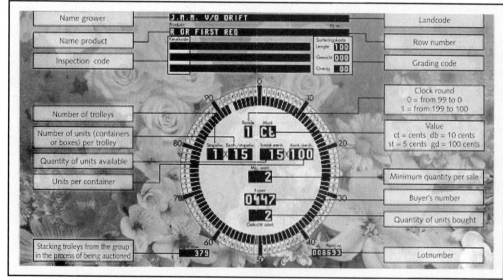

Figure 2.4

Computerized Auction clock for Dutch Flower Auctions

Source: aquarius-flora.com (see Auction, introduction)

- Sellers list a starting price for one item, and the number of items for sale.
- If no bids are made, the starting price is reduced.
- Bidders specify both a bid price and the quantity they want to buy.
- All winning bidders pay the **same** price per item, which is the lowest successful bid. This might be less than what you bid!
- If there are more buyers than items, the earliest successful bids get the goods.
- Higher bidders are more likely to get the quantities they've requested.
- Proxy bidding is not used in Dutch auctions.

- Bidders can refuse partial quantities. For example, if you place a bid for ten items and only eight are available after the auction, you don't have to buy any of them.

Free-Fall (Declining Price) Auction

This is a variation of the Dutch auction in which only one item is auctioned at a time. The price starts at a very high level, and then it is reduced at fixed time intervals until a bid is offered and becomes the winning bid. This type of auction is used with popular items, where many bidders are expected; the freefall auction moves very fast in such a case.

3. **One buyer, many potential sellers.** In this case one uses a **reverse auction** approach, also known as a *bidding or tendering system*. In a reverse auction, an item the buyer needs is placed on an RFQ. Potential sellers bid on the job, reducing the price sequentially. In electronic biddings, several rounds of bidding take place until the bidders no longer reduce the price. The winner is the one with the lowest bid, if only price is considered. Because this is primarily a B2B or G2B mechanism, other criteria are considered and the winner is selected from a group of, say, the five lower bids.

4. **Many sellers, many buyers.** In this case, *buyers and their bidding prices* and *sellers and their asking prices* are matched, considering the quantities on both sides. Stocks and commodities markets are typical examples. Buyers and sellers can be individuals or businesses. Such auctions are called **double auctions**.

Sealed-Bid First-Price Auction

You bid only once in this type of auction. It is a silent auction and the bidders do not know who is placing bids or what the prices are. The item is awarded to the highest bidder.

Sealed-Bid Second-Price Auction (Vickrey Auction)

The item is awarded to the highest bidder, but at the second-highest bid. This is done to alleviate bidders' fears of significantly exceeding the true market value.

Again, we assume that each bidder submits one bid without knowing the other bids. This method is not used much on the Internet. The reason is that most Internet auctions are not sealed. Actually, Web technology facilitates disclosure of prices, as in the English model. For further details and discussion, including bidding strategies, see Vakrat and Seidmann (2000).

2.3 Benefits, Limitations, and Economic Impacts

Electronic auctions are becoming important selling and buying channels for many companies and individuals. E-auctions enable buyers to access goods and services anywhere auctions are conducted. Moreover almost perfect market information is available about prices, products, current supply and demand, and so on. These characteristics provide benefits to all.

BENEFITS TO SELLERS

- Increased revenues by broadening customer base and shortening cycle time. With e-auctions, sellers can reach the most interested buyers in the most efficient way and sell at a price equal to buyer valuation of the product. This eliminates the need to predict demand and the risk of pricing items too high or too low.
- Optimal price setting. Sellers can make use of the information collected about price sensitivity to set prices in other fixed-price markets.
- Disintermediation. Sellers can gain more customer dollars by offering items directly, rather than going through an expensive intermediary or by using an expensive physical auction.
- Better customer relationships. Buyers and sellers have more chances and time to interact with each other, thus creating a sense of community and loyalty.

Additionally, by making use of the information gathered on customer interests, sellers can improve the overall e-commerce experiences of buyers and can deliver more personalized content to buyers, thus enhancing customer relationships.

- Liquidation. Sellers can liquidate large quantities of obsolete items very quickly.

BENEFITS TO BUYERS

- Opportunities to find unique items and collectibles.
- Chance to bargain. Instead of buying at a fixed price, the bidding mechanism allows buyers to bargain with sellers at their desired prices.
- Entertainment. Participating in e-auctions can be entertaining and exciting. The interaction between buyers and sellers may create goodwill and positive feelings, and buyers can interact as little or as much as they like.
- Anonymity. With the help of a third party, buyers can remain anonymous.
- Convenience. Buyers can trade from anywhere, even with a cell phone.

BENEFITS TO E-AUCTIONEERS

- Higher repeat purchase rate. Jupiter Communications conducted a study in 1998 that shows comparative repeat-purchase rates across some of the top e-commerce sites. The findings indicate that auction sites such as eBay and uBid tend to garner higher repeat-purchase rates than the top e-commerce B2C sites, such as Amazon.com.
- More "sticky" Web sites. **"Stickiness"** refers to the tendency of customers to stay at (auction) Web sites longer and come back more. Auction sites are frequently "stickier" than fixed-priced sites. With sticky sites, more advertising revenue can be generated because of more impressions and longer viewing times.
- Expansion of the auction business. An example of how auctioneers can expand their business can be seen in the example of Manheim Auctions (Mckeown and Watson, [1999]). Manheim Auctions, the world's largest auction house, created Manheim Online (MOL) in 1999 to sell program cars (cars that have been previously leased or hired) in response to the Japanese company Aucnet's efforts to penetrate the U.S. car auction business. This Internet-based electronic sales system has tremendous potential to change the car auction business. There are over 80,000 used car dealers in the United States, and Manheim auctions some 6 million cars for them each year. Trying to leverage its knowledge of the automobile market to provide services to its customers, Manheim developed two other products, Manheim Market Report and AutoConnect. It is also expanding its auction business in Europe. Manheim wants to continue to add value to Manheim Online as a way of discouraging competition and of extending sales through the Internet without cannibalizing Manheim's core business.

LIMITATIONS

E-auctions have several limitations, including the following:

- **Possibility of fraud.** Auction items are in many cases unique, used, or antique. Since one cannot see the item, you may get a defective product. Also, buyers can commit fraud; thus, the fraud rate is very high. (For specific fraud techniques and how to prevent them, see Section 2.8.)
- **Limited participation.** Some auctions are by invitation only, while others are open to dealers only, so they are not open to all.
- **Security.** Some of the C2C auctions conducted on the Internet are not secure. On the other hand, some B2B auctions are conducted on highly secure private lines.
- **Software.** Unfortunately, there are only a few "complete" or "off-the-shelf" market-enabling solutions that can support the dynamic commerce functionality required for optimizing pricing strategies *and* that can be easily customized to the unique requirements of a company or industry. In short, dynamic commerce "best practices" are still being defined within industries and will continue to evolve as new business processes emerge online.

STRATEGIC USES OF AUCTIONS AND PRICING MECHANISMS

By utilizing dynamic pricing, buyers and suppliers are able to optimize product inventory levels and adjust pricing strategies very quickly. For example, by using Web-based auctions and exchanges, suppliers can quickly flush excess inventory and liquidate idle assets. Buyers may end up with the power to procure goods and services at the prices they desire. The endgame is to accurately assess and exploit market supply and demand requirements faster and more efficiently than the competition.

Aberdeen Research (2000) showed that market-makers leveraging auction exchange models are reaching "liquidity" (critical mass) more rapidly than those utilizing only catalog-order–based trading environments. However, businesses are still struggling to understand how to truly implement dynamic pricing models to augment existing business practices.

One suggestion of how to do it was provided by Westland (2000), who observed that e-auctions place much more power in the hands of the consumer than e-tailing. He suggested that the following 10 lessons can be learned from stock exchanges for e-tailing auctions:

Lesson 1: Customers are attracted to e-auction markets because they provide greater liquidity than traditional markets; ceteris paribus, this greater liquidity results directly from greater geographical reach provided to commercial transactions by electronic networks.

Lesson 2: Electronic auction markets can more efficiently discover the best price at which to trade in a product.

Lesson 3: Electronic auction markets can, at low cost, provide exceptional levels of transparency of both market operations and product quality.

Lesson 4: Electronic auction markets are more efficient than traditional markets. This efficiency allows e-auctions to better provide information required to correctly price assets traded in the marketplace.

Lesson 5: Electronic auctions can provide a market that, ceteris paribus, offers services at a lower transaction cost.

Lesson 6: Customers will abandon a market that is not perceived as fair, even though they may initially profit from "unfair" transactions in that market. By distancing customers from the traders in a market, they can provide a false sense of legitimacy to a market that allows unfair and opaque trading practices.

Lesson 7: Electronic auction systems must manage all aspects of trading activity, from initiation to settlement and delivery. Markets that fail to integrate both price discovery and order completion (settlement) into their operations can encourage unfair trading behavior, and opaque trading practices.

Lesson 8: Because the delay in price response may result in significantly faster completion and posting times, there is greater potential for feedback loops and instabilities that are a threat to orderly trading, and to fair and efficient pricing of assets traded.

Lesson 9: Electronic auctions may fuel unfair trading practices through different relative speeds of service through different parts of its network linking trading to customers.

Lesson 10: Order-driven e-auction markets demand that markets clearly define when a sale has been made.

IMPACTS

Because the trade objects and contexts for auctions are very diverse, the economic rationale behind auctions and the motives of the different participants to set up auctions are quite different. Representative impacts include the following:

AUCTIONS AS A COORDINATION MECHANISM. Auctions are increasingly used as an efficient coordination mechanism for establishing an equilibrium in price. An example is auctions for the allocation of telecommunication bandwidth. In these auctions there is little or no human intervention during the trading process.

Reverse Mortgage Auctions in Singapore

Homebuyers like to get the lowest possible mortgage rates. In the US, Priceline.com will try to find you a mortgage if you "name your own price." However, a better deal may be available to homebuyers in Singapore, where reverse auctions are combined with "group purchasing," saving about $20,000 over the life of a mortgage, for each homeowner, plus $1,200 in waived legal fees.

Dollardex.com offers the service in Singapore, Hong Kong, and other countries. As of Spring 2000, in addition to mortgages the site offers car loans, insurance policies and other financial services. Here is how the site arranged its first project:

The site invited potential buyers in three residential properties in Singapore, to join the service. Applications were made on a secure Web site, including financial credentials. Then, seven lending banks were invited to bid on the loans.

In a secure electronic room borrowers and lenders negotiated. After two days of negotiations of interest rates and special conditions, the borrowers voted on one bank. In the first project, 18 borrowers agreed to give the job to UOB, paying about .5% less than the regular rates. The borrowers negotiated the waiver of the legal fee as well. UOB generated $10 million of business. Today, customers can participate in an individual reverse auction if they do not want to join a group.

The banks can see the offers made by the competitors. Flexibility is high, in addition to interest rates, down payment size, switching from a fixed to variable rate options, etc., are also negotiated. On the average, there are 2.6 bank bids per customer.

The site offers matching services for travel and insurance. It also allows comparisons of mutual funds that agreed to give lower front-end fees.

Sources: Compiled from the *Asian Wall Street Journal*, March 14-15, 2000, and from dollardex.com.

AUCTIONS AS A SOCIAL MECHANISM TO DETERMINE A PRICE. For objects not being traded in traditional markets, such as unique or rare items, or for items that may be offered randomly, or at long intervals, an auction creates a marketplace that attracts potential buyers, and often experts. By offering many of these special items at a single time, and by attracting considerable attention, auctions provide the requisite exposure of purchase and sale orders and hence liquidity of the market in which a price can be determined. Typical examples are auctions of fine arts or rare items, as well as auctions of communication frequencies, Web banners, and advertising space. For example, winebid.com is a global site of auctions for wine collectors.

AUCTIONS AS A HIGHLY VISIBLE DISTRIBUTION MECHANISM. Another type of auction is similar to the previous one, but it deals with special offers. In this case, the setup of the auction is different: Typically, one supplier auctions off a limited amount of items, using the auction primarily as a mechanism to gain attention and to attract those customers who are bargain hunters or have a preference for the gambling dimension of the auction process. The airline-seat auctions by Cathy Pacific, American Airlines, and Lufthansa fall into this category.

AUCTION AS A COMPONENT IN E-COMMERCE. Auctions can stand alone, or they can be combined with other e-commerce activities. An example is combining group purchasing with reverse auctions (see Application Case 2.1).

Some of the impacts of electronic auctions are presented in Figure 2.5. The figure shows the components of the auctions, the participants, and the process. The impacts are summarized in Table 2.2.

2.4   The "Name-Your-Own-Price" C2B Model

One of the most interesting models of e-commerce is known as the **"name-your-own-price"** model. This model appears in several variations and is associated with Priceline.com.

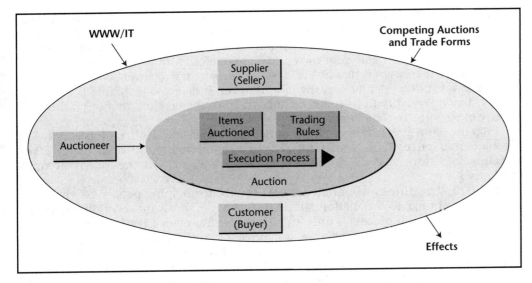

Figure 2.5

The Components of Auctions

Source: Modified from Klein (1997), p. 4.

Table 2.2

Summary of Impact Areas

Parameter	Impact of the Web
Auctioneer	Lower entry barriers; opportunity for direct sales
Access rules	Customizable; theoretically millions of potential customers can be reached
Items auctioned	Focused product segments can be auctioned off; the technology extends the complexity of the product description.
Trading rules	The trading rules reflect the lack of a guaranteed service.
Execution process	For digital products the entire trading cycle can be handled on the Web; for physical products the trading process and the physical logistics of the trade objects can be separated, leading to a reduction of costs.

Source: Modified from Klein (1997), p. 5.

THE PRICELINE MODEL

Priceline.com pioneered the "name-your-own-price" concept and the "name-your-own-price" Internet pricing system that enables consumers to achieve significant savings by naming their own price for goods and services. Therefore, it is basically a consumer-to-business (C2B) model. Priceline.com either presents consumer offers to sellers who can fill as much of that guaranteed demand as they wish at "price points" requested by buyers, or searches a Priceline.com database that contains vendors' minimum prices and tries to match supply against requests. In short, Priceline.com's "virtual" business model allows for rapid scaling, using the Internet for collecting consumer demand and trying to fill it. The approach is based on the fundamental concept of the downward-sloping demand curve in which prices vary based on demand. For example, airlines have about 500,000 empty seats every day.

The company is currently selling multiple products and services mainly across the following product categories: a travel service that offers leisure airline tickets, hotel rooms and rented cars, a personal finance service that offers home refinancing and home equity loans, and an automotive service that offers new cars. New services that were added in 2000 include credit cards and long-distance calling. In 2000 the company teamed up with Hutchison Whampoa Limited, one of Asia's largest owners of telecommunications and Internet infrastructure, to offer a range of services in Asia, including China and Hong Kong, India, Taiwan, Indonesia, Singapore, Thailand, Korea, Malaysia, the Philippines, and Vietnam. Priceline.com also has offices in many other countries.

According to the market research firm Opinion Research Corporation International of Princeton, Priceline.com is the Internet's second most-recognized e-commerce brand behind Amazon.com. Two-thirds of all adults in the United States have heard of Priceline.com and its "name-your-own-price" commercial formula.

Basically, the concept is that of a C2B *reverse auction,* in which vendors submit offers and the lowest-priced vendor gets the job; however, if database matching is done, the activity may not qualify to be called an auction since the vendors are not placing bids directly in response to a customer request.

Priceline.com asks customers to guarantee acceptance of the offer if it is at or below the requested price. This is guaranteed by giving a credit card number. In 2000, Priceline.com suspended the delivery of food, gasoline, and groceries due to accumulated losses.

In 2000, Priceline.com initiated a new service for helping people get rid of old things. It is similar to an auction site with heavy emphasis on secondhand goods. However, the auction process is different. The new site, named Perfect YardSale, lets a user make an offer below the seller's asking price for an item, a system that's similar to the haggling that goes on at garage and yard sales. Also, the buyer and seller are expected to meet face-to-face. Priceline.com argues that its method leads to bargains for buyers that are better than at auctions, where the highest bidder wins. So buyers and sellers can swap goods in person, eliminating the expense of shipping. Perfect YardSale transactions are limited to local metropolitan areas.

Jay Walker, vice chairman and founder of Priceline.com, said he expects Perfect YardSale to attract a different type of merchant: the individual seller seeking to get rid of unwanted possessions on the cheap. In contrast, he argues, much of the trade on Internet auction sites is conducted by dealers selling the hottest new toys, antiques, and other collectibles. These items are not available on Perfect YardSale.

The system works like this: A buyer hunting for a digital camera, for example, selects the features he or she wants on Perfect YardSale, the price he or she is willing to pay, and how long he or she wants the site to search for a seller that meets his demands. The buyer will then be required to submit a credit-card number to demonstrate that his bid is serious.

Once Perfect YardSale finds a willing seller, the two parties arrange to meet so the buyer can inspect the merchandise. If the buyer is satisfied with the condition of the item, he'll give the seller a secret pass-code. The seller can then enter the pass-code into the Perfect YardSale site to receive payment for the item directly from Priceline and the buyer can take the purchased item.

Unfortunately, Perfect YardSale terminated its services in October 2000 due to cash shortage of Priceline.com.

OTHER MODELS

Several similar models are offered by competitors. For example, Savvio.com offers a model for travelers that combines a real-time declining-price auction and full disclosure of itinerary details on discounted international and domestic air travel and cruise tickets. Unlike "name-your-own-price" travel sites, Savvio.com allows consumers to view the airline, flight number, aircraft type, exact departure and arrival times, and ticket availability before purchasing tickets.

TravelBids.com allows travelers to place an RFQ, then TravelBids asks vendors to bid on it. The site is similar to Priceline.com, except that it uses only auctions (see the comparison with Priceline.com available on the TravelBids.com site).

2.5 The Auction Process and Software Support

A number of software or intelligent tools are available to help buyers and sellers to find an auction or complete a transaction. The sellers and buyers usually go through a four-phase process: searching and comparing, getting started for an auction, actual bidding, and post-auction activities (see Figure 2.6).

There are several support tools for each phase. Let's explore them, by the auction phase where they are used.

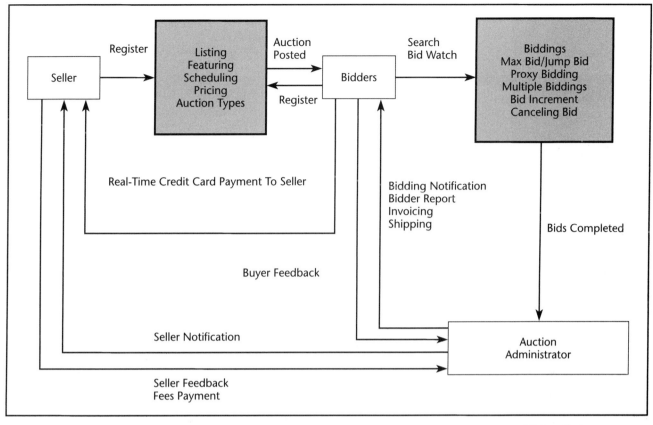

Figure 2.6

The Process of E-auction

PHASE 1: SEARCHING AND COMPARING

Auctions are conducted on hundreds of sites worldwide. Therefore, sellers and buyers need to execute extensive searches and comparisons to select desirable auction locations. The following support tools may be of interest to them:

Mega-Searching and Comparisons

Many Web sites offer links to hundreds of auction sites, or they provide search tools for specific sites. The mega-searching utility not only helps sellers find suitable locations to list their items, but it also enables buyers to browse available auction sites efficiently (see Application Case 2.2). Popular searching tools include the following:

- **Auction Watch** (AuctionWatch.com) contains a directory of auction sites organized by categories, as well as auction news, message boards, and more.
- **The Internet Auction List** (Internetauctionlist.com) is packed with news about e-auctions worldwide and features access to innumerable specialty auctions.
- **Yahoo!'s Auction List** (auctions.yahoo.com) contains a list of over 400 auction-related links.
- **BidStream** (Bidstream.com from opensiteauction.com) conducts multiple auction searches and finds out which site is selling similar items.
- **Bidder's Edge** (Biddersedge.com) conducts searches across multiple auction houses for specific auction products and pricing information. It provides detailed historical information on items that have appeared for sale before.
- **Itrack** (Itrack.com) searches eBay, Yahoo, and Amazon for specific items that users designate.
- **Turbobid** (Turbobid.com) provides a mega-search service that helps local bidders look for items they want from a pool of e-auction sites in Hong Kong.

Finding When and Where an Item is Auctioned

This is the process that Efraim Turban went through:

1. Enter **biddersedge.com**
2. Request "Pool Table" on the Keyword option

This search engine claims that they search at more than 200 auction sites.

The search found 63 auctions, which are organized as shown in the table below (a sample).

I was able to sort the auctions by:

Type of seller ("Buy Type"), retailer, person to person (P2P), fixed price etc. I noticed that eBay was not on the list, probably because of the reasons cited in application case 2.3.

Next, I went to matching categories. I decided to match the pool table with "jewelry." I found several matches in which people were selling a pool table and some jewelry together.

Then I noticed that I could try the same search at eBay. So, I went there and found 15 items such as pool tables, charms and rings. Some of the items were new and at a fixed price.

At that time I had an option to add the search to my personal shopper page.

Next I was looking for a "Boeing 777." I found an auction for a Herpa Wings, Emirates Boeing 777-200, for $18. This was of course not a real plane. So, I registered with the auction tracker that promised to track the airplane for me, and with "ping me," a free service that promised to send me a notification alert. There was no pricing history on the Boeing 777, nor on a pool table. But I found lots of price history on Barbie Dolls, including price ranges at different times the last 12 months. Finally the site had a notice about the company relationship with eBay, including the legal situation (see Application case 2.3).

Toys & Beanies>Plush>Other	Auction Site =Trusted	Price (approx.)	Close (ETS) Change zone	Buy Type
Hardvard 8' Oakwood Slatron Pool Table w/Ball Return & FREE SHIPPING!	EGGHEAD.com	$745.99	03/05, 05:52PM	Retailer
Voit Competition Table Soccer (New)	EGGHEAD.com	$79.99	04/11, 01:00PM	Retailer
Executive-Size Pool Table/Billiards Set	BidBay	$95.00	02/01, 09:06PM	P2P
Peter Sellers~Pool~Pool Table~ 16"x 20" Poster	Amazon	$18.95	02/05, 12:44AM	P2P

Automated Search Services

Automated search services notify buyers when items they are interested in are available at one or several auction sites. Buyers need to complete a simple form specifying the item, then search for assistance tools such as Auction Watchers, BidFind, BidStream, and iTract will keep tabs on auction sites and notify buyers by e-mail. The Notify Me When PersonalShopper assists bidders only at eBay.

Automated search engines at auction site entrances are beneficial to users but may not be appreciated by the auction site (see Application Case 2.3).

Browsing Site Categories

Almost all auction-site home pages contain a directory of categories. Buyers can browse the category and its subcategories to narrow the search. Some sites also enable users to sort items according to the time a specific auction is conducted.

Basic and Advanced Searching

Buyers can use search engines to look for a single term, multiple terms, or key words. To conduct an advanced search, buyers can fill in a search form to specify search titles, item

Issue in Auction Aggregation

In September 1999, eBay initiated drastic policy against third parties "predatory" search agents. These agents enter the major online auction sites and search items consumers are looking for, notifying consumers when an auction is done and where. The policy prohibits the third party search sites from collecting and sharing information found on eBay's site. The problem, as reported, was that the search agents were frequently accessing eBay, sifting through auction offers, harvesting the information and placing it on alternate Web sites, such as biddersEdge.com, AuctionWatch.com, AuctionRover.com, itrack.com and Ruby Lane. EBay claimed that these search agents were harmful in multiple ways. First they would slow down eBay's transaction processing systems, thus reducing performance for all other eBay visitors. Second, outside search agents might not show the most up-to-date information and thus lower auction users' purchasing experience. Executives from the third party companies were quick to point out that their systems were actually benevolent in that they served as "repeaters" or mirrors of eBay's information, thus actually lowering the load. Furthermore, they stressed that actual purchases were after all carried out at eBay's site, so that business was not really taken away from the company, and that in fact, they bring more bidders to eBay.

The culprits in this situation were mobile intelligent agents, intelligent agents that can interact with hosts' computers other than the one they originate on, move from host to host, and extract and store data in the process. In the eBay scenario, they were "harvesting" information and were sending it to their company's computer which collected, analyzed, and re-distributed that information.

Are agents truly culprits or predators as suggested? EBay's response clearly suggests so, as do several of the readers' comments following the policy announcement. Yet, Murch and Johnson (1999) are claiming just the opposite, stating, "It is in the interest of all companies that wish to sell over the Internet...that their information is formatted and available in such a way that it can be easily accessed by...these agents." In other words, agents are viewed by some as having positive characteristics. This incident created a debate in chat rooms and newsgroups (e.g., see "talkback post" at znet.com). Most customers criticized eBay. In early 2000, eBay licensed AuctionRover to aggregate auctions from eBay. AuctionRover had similar agreements with dozens of other auction sites.

---

descriptions, sellers' IDs, auction item numbers, price ranges, locations, closing dates, completed auctions, and so forth.

PHASE 2: GETTING STARTED AT AN AUCTION

To participate in an auction, one needs to register at the selected site. After registration, sellers can list, feature, schedule, and price their items on the site. Buyers can check sellers' profiles and other details—such as the minimum bid amount, the auction policy, and the payment method allowed—then place their bids.

Registration and Profiling

Sellers and buyers must register their names, user IDs, and passwords before they can start participating at a specific auction. The user's page header and the auction listing will display a basic description of sellers and their listings. Before submitting a bid, buyers can check a seller's profile, including information such as membership IDs and previous transaction records. If the auction site provides voluntary verified-user programs such as BidSafe (auctions.cnet.com), buyers can check whether sellers are qualified auction community members as verified by the third-party security source.

Listing and Promoting

Several software programs can help sellers to list and promote their items.

- **Advertisement Wizard** (see samcool.com, Websabre.com). Helps users in creating attractive advertisements and auction postings. With a simple-to-use, fill-in-the-blank interface, users can create great-looking advertisements for e-auctions.

- **Auction Assistant** (see backthornesw.com, tucows.com). This tool and Ad Studio (adstudio.net) help in creating auction listings, changing a font, adding a background, selecting a theme, and including standard details, such as shipping policy and payment terms. The tools also can be used to track sales, payments, and shipping.
- **Auction Poster98** (see auctionposter.com). This program makes it simple to add pictures, and it interacts directly with eBay. It helps in adding backgrounds, photos, etc., without design or programming skills. The program can create up to 100 ads at a time, and it supports bulk listing.
- **Auction Wizard** (see mr-wizard.com). This program can upload up to 100 items simultaneously. It is an auction-posting tool that saves cutting and pasting. Auction Wizard also enters user ID, password, auction title, location, opening bid, category, and auction duration.
- **Mister Lister on eBay** (see ebay.com/services/buyandsell). Sellers can upload many items at one time.
- **Bulk Loader** (see Yahoo Auctions). Seller can load several auctions into a spreadsheet program like Microsoft Excel.

Pricing

To post an item for biddings, sellers have to decide the minimum bid amount, the bid increment, and any *reserve price* (the lowest price for which a seller is willing to sell an item). Sellers can search for *comparable guides* with Web search engines like BidFind.com, BottomDollar.com, PriceScan.com, and AuctionWatch.com. If an auction site allows searching for auctions closed in the past, the transacted prices of similar items can provide a benchmark for a buyer's bidding strategy or a minimum acceptable price for a seller.

PHASE 3: THE ACTUAL BIDDING

In the bidding phase, buyers can submit bids themselves or make use of software tools that place bids on their behalf. They can also use tools to view the bidding status and to place bids across different sites in real time.

Bid Watching and Multiple Biddings

Buyers can visit the user page of an e-auction Web site at any time and keep track of the status of active auctions. They can review bids and auctions they are currently winning or losing or have recently won. Tools provided in the United States by BidWatch (egghead.com), Bid Monitor (bruceclay.com), and EasyScreen Layout (auctionbroker.com) allow bidders to view their bids across different auction sites in an organized way. Bidders can also place their bids at multiple auction sites using a single screen without switching from one window to another.

Auto-Snipping

Snipping is the act of entering a bid during the very last seconds of an auction and outbidding the highest bidder. Auction Express offers a tool (auctiontool.com) to help buyers to snip items automatically.

eProxy Biddings

A software system can operate as a proxy to place bids on behalf of buyers. In such **proxy bidding** a buyer should determine his or her *maximum bid,* then place the first bid manually. The proxy will then execute the bids, trying to keep the bids as low as possible. When someone enters a new bid, the proxy automatically will raise the bid to the next level until it reaches the predetermined maximum price. This function is not applicable in a Dutch auction in which prices are decreasing.

PHASE 4: POST-AUCTION FOLLOW-UP

When auctions are completed, post-auction activities take place. These include e-mail notifications and arrangements for payment and shipping. A typical post-auction tool is Easy! Auction (saveeasy.com).

Post-Auction Notifications

- **Bidding Notifications.** Buyers receive e-mail messages or beeper messages notifying them while the bidding is going on (English bidding), each time they are being outbid or winning an auction.
- **End-of-Auction Notices.** When an auction closes, sellers receive e-mail messages naming the highest bidder. End-of-auction e-mails provide seller and buyer IDs, seller and winner e-mail addresses, a link to the auction ad, auction title or item name, final price, auction ending date and time, total number of bids, and the starting and highest bid amounts.
- **Seller Notices.** After an auction ends, the seller generally contacts the buyer. Seller notices typically provide auction number and item name, total purchase price (winning bid plus shipping), payment preferences, mailing address, etc.
- **Postcards and Thank-you Notes.** AuctionWatch.com helps sellers create a customized close-of-auction or thank-you note for winning bidders.

User Communication

User-to-user online communication appears in a number of forms:

- **Chat Groups.** Areas on e-auction sites and auction-related sites, where people can post messages in real time to get quick feedback from others.
- **Mailing Lists.** A group of people talking about a chosen topic via e-mail messages.
- **Message Boards.** Areas on e-auction sites and auction-related sites where people can post messages that other users can read at their convenience. Other message board participants can post replies for all to read.

Feedback and Rating

Most e-auction sites provide a feedback and rating feature that enables auction community members to monitor each other. This feature enables users to rank sellers or bidders and add short comments about sellers, bidders, and transactions.

Invoicing and Billing

An invoicing utility tool can e-mail and print one or all invoices, search and arrange invoices in a number of ways, edit invoices, and delete invoices. This utility automatically calculates shipping charges and sales tax. It can also automatically calculate and charge the seller with the listing fees and/or a percentage of the sale as commission.

Payment Methods

Sellers and winning bidders can arrange payment to be made by such methods as cashier's check, C.O.D. (cash on delivery), credit card, electronic transfer, and an escrow service. A number of online services are available for electronic transfer, escrow services, and credit-card payment, such as the following:

- **Electronic Transfer Service.** Buyers can pay electronically via PayByWeb.com, Paypal.com, or BidPay.com.
- **Escrow Service.** An independent third party holds a bidder's payment in trust until the buyer receives and accepts the auction item from the seller. This service charges a fee and is usually reserved for high-end transactions. Examples of escrow service providers include i-Escrow (iescrow.com), tradenable.com, TradeSafe.com, and insuredeal.com.

- **Credit-Card Payment.** Billpoint.com or CCNow.com services facilitate person-to-person credit-card transactions. Billpoint's payment processing system offers many of the same protections as escrow, such as payment processing, shipment tracking, and fraud protection.

Shipping and Postage

- **Internet Shippers.** Shipping providers such as Iship.com, Smartship.com, and AuctionShip.com help sellers by providing a one-stop integrated service for processing, shipping, and packing e-commerce goods.
- **Internet Postage.** Postage service providers such as Stamp.com and E-stamp.com allow users to download postage, print "stamped" envelopes and labels, and arrange shipments via the U.S. Postal Service. These providers charge sellers both fixed and transaction fees for the services. For further details see auctiontool.com.

ADDITIONAL TERMS AND RULES

Each auction house has its own rules and guides. The following are some examples:

- **Reserve Price Auction.** This is the lowest price for which a seller is willing to sell an item.
- **Vertical Auction.** Specialized auctions, sometimes referred to as "auction vortals." They are particularly useful in B2B. At eBay anything goes, but many auction sites specialize in one area. For example, TechSmart Inc. specializes in selling used or outdated PCs in B2B auctions.
- **Bid Retraction.** Refers to cancellation of a bid by a bidder, and it is used only in special circumstances. Usually a bid is considered to be a binding contract.
- **Featured Auctions.** These get extra exposure when they are listed in Web sites. Sellers pay extra for this service.

2.6 Auctions on Private Networks

Electronic auctions that run on private networks have been in use for about 15 years. The following are B2B examples.

PIGS IN SINGAPORE AND TAIWAN. Pig auctioning in Singapore (see Neo 1992) and Taiwan has been conducted on private networks for more than 10 years. Growers bring the pigs to one area, where they are washed, weighed, and prepared for display. The pigs are auctioned (forward auction) one at a time, while all the data about them is displayed to about 40 approved bidders who bid on a displayed price. If bids are submitted, the price is increased by 20 cents per kilogram. The process continues until no one bids. A computer monitors the bidders' financial capability (in other words, the computer verifies that the bidder has available funds in the prepaid account that was opened for the auction).

CARS IN JAPAN—AUCNET. Started in Japan, Aucnet began auctioning used cars to dealers on television in the mid-1980s. In 1992 it opened Aucnet USA Inc. and started auctioning cars in the United States. In 1996 Aucnet moved to a private network, and in 1998 it moved to the Internet, expanding to flowers, antiques, and more. In 1998 Aucnet USA was closed. Today, in Japan, Aucnet also auctions computer hardware and software and provides services such as insurance and leasing. (For further details, see aucnet.co.jp/english.)

LIVESTOCK IN AUSTRALIA. ComputerAided Livestock Marketing (CALM) is an electronic online system for trading cattle and sheep. It has been in operation since 1986, and in contrast with the pigs system in Singapore, livestock does not have to travel to CALM, which lowers the stress in the animals and reduces costs. The buyers use PCs or

Vt100 terminals. The system also handles payments to farmers. (For further details, see anu.edu.au/people/Roger.Clarke/EC/CALM.)

2.7 Double Auctions, Bundle Trading, and Pricing Issues

DOUBLE AUCTIONS

Auctions can be **single auctions,** where either an item is offered for sale and the market consists of multiple buyers making bids to buy, or an item is wanted and the market consists of multiple sellers, making offers to sell. In either case, one side of the market consists of a single entity. On the other hand, multiple buyers and sellers may be making bids and offers simultaneously in a **double auction.** An example of a double auction is stock trading.

Although most online auctions are single, double auctions are important for certain types of transactions. Their procedures and market-clearing level of price are unique.

In a double auction, multiple units of product may be auctioned off at the same time. The situation will get complicated when the quantity offered is more than one and buyers and sellers bid on varying quantities.

In a given trading period, any seller may make an offer while any buyer makes a bid. Either a seller or a buyer may accept the offer or bid any time. The difference between cost and price paid is the seller's profit; the difference between price paid and valuation is the buyer's surplus. If the quantities vary, as in a stock market, a market maker needs to match quantities as well.

Prices in Double Auctions

According to Choi and Whinston (2000), double auction markets tend to generate competitive outcomes. Simply put, a double auction is an interactive form of market in which both buyers and sellers are competitive. In contrast, in a single auction contract prices may be much higher or much lower than in a competitive level. This conclusion will have a significant effect on the future use of double auctions in the digital economy.

Ideally, any effort to promote competitiveness should include expanding double auctions and similar market mechanisms as they offer an opportunity to raise economic efficiencies unsurpassed by any physical market organization. For auctioneers, however, single auctions generate substantially more revenue than double auctions.

BUNDLE TRADING

One of the major characteristics of the digital economy is the personalization and customization of products and services. This often means a collection of complementary goods and services. A combination of airline tickets, hotel rooms, a rental car, meals, and amusement park admission tickets can be bundled as a packaged leisure product. Some products that are vertically related (e.g., a computer operating system and a Web browser) may be provided by different vendors, requiring buyers to deal with multiple sellers. While a purchase that involves multiple sellers may be carried out through a series of transactions or auctions, bundle trading offers a simplified and efficient alternative solution.

The management and operation of a bundle market is complex, and it differs considerably from those of single or double auction markets. For a discussion see Choi and Whinston (2000).

PRICES IN AUCTIONS: HIGHER OR LOWER?

Compared to competitive markets, prices in auctions tend to be higher, reaching monopoly level when there is only one seller (Choi and Whinston, 2000). In general, the auctioneer is in a better position to maximize revenues. When the auctioneer is selling a product among multiple bidders, the expected price is often higher than the competitive level. Conversely, when the auctioneer is buying from multiple offers, he or she may choose the lowest offer, which is usually lower than the competitive market price. This result is largely due to the simple fact that there is competition among bidders.

However, in many instances prices in auctions are lower. This may happen in cases of liquidation, where the seller's objective is to sell as quickly as possible. Alternatively, buyers go to global markets where they can get products more cheaply than if imported by intermediaries. In general, buyers expect online prices to be lower. For example, truckers or airlines selling unused capacity at the last minute usually do so at a lower price. Also, considering the fact that most C2C auctions are for used merchandise, and surplus B2B auctions may include used or obsolete products, bargain prices are likely to prevail.

Finally, a more fundamental reason for lower online auction prices, is that an online auction is usually an alternative selling channel, instead of being an exclusive selling arrangement. Therefore, buyers can always revert to physical markets if bids exceed posted prices. In short, no one is willing to pay what they are expected to pay in physical markets. If products are sold exclusively through online auctions, the average price will certainly increase.

PRICING STRATEGIES IN ONLINE AUCTIONS

Both sellers and buyers may develop strategies for auctioning. Sellers have the option to use different mechanisms, such as English, Dutch, sealed-bid first price, and sealed-bid second price. Buyers need to develop a strategy regarding how much to increase a bid and when to stop bidding. These topics are relevant to offline auctions as well and will not be dealt with here.

2.8 Fraud in Auctions and Its Prevention

According to Internet Fraud Watch (fraud.org/internet), among all e-commerce activities conducted over the Internet, fraud is most serious in e-auctions. It accounted for 87 percent of the e-commerce fraud that occurred in 1999. According to the National Consumer League's National Fraud Information Center, 9 out of 10 registered Internet-related complaints are concerned with auction fraud. The average auction loss is $248 per complaint, and roughly $1.1 million was lost due to fraudulent activity in 1999.

In October 2000, Amazon.com cancelled the auctions of World Series tickets because of extensive speculation that violated the New York State law that prohibits selling tickets for $5 or 10 percent more than face value.

TYPES OF E-AUCTION FRAUD

Fraud may be conducted by sellers or by buyers. The following are some examples:

BID SHIELDING. Bid shielding is the use of phantom bidders to bid at a very high price when an auction begins. The phantom bidders pull out at the last minute, and the bidder who bids with a very low price wins. The bogus bidders were the shields, protecting the low bid of the third bidder in the stack. By bid shielding, a ring of dishonest bidders can target an item and inflate the bid value to scare off other real bidders.

SHILLING. Sellers arrange to have fake bids placed on their items (either by associates or by using multiple user IDs) to artificially jack up high bids. If they see a legitimate high bid that doesn't meet their expectations as the end of an auction draws near, they might pop in to manipulate the price.

FAKE PHOTOS AND MISLEADING DESCRIPTIONS. In reaching for bidders' attention, some sellers distort what they can truly sell. Borrowed images, ambiguous descriptions, and falsified facts are some of the tactics that sellers might employ.

IMPROPER GRADING TECHNIQUES. Grading items is often the most hotly debated issue among buyers and sellers. The seller might describe an item as 90 percent new while the bidder, after receiving the item and paying the full amount, feels it is only 70 percent new. Condition is often in the eye of the beholder. Although many grading systems have been devised and put to use, condition is still subject to interpretation.

SELLING REPRODUCTIONS. A seller sells something that he claims is original, but it turns out to be a reproduction.

HIGH SHIPPING COSTS AND HANDLING FEES. Some sellers just want to get a little more cash out of bidders. Postage and handling rates vary from seller to seller. Some charge extra to cover "handling" costs and other overhead intangibles, while others charge to cover the cost of packaging supplies, even though such supplies are often available for free.

FAILURE TO SHIP MERCHANDISE. It's the old collect-and-run routine. Money was paid out but the merchandise never arrived.

LOSS AND DAMAGE CLAIMS. Buyers claim they never received an item or received it in damaged condition and they ask for a refund. They might be trying to get a freebie. The seller sometimes can't prove whether the item ever arrived or whether it was in perfect condition when shipped.

SWITCH AND RETURN. The seller has successfully auctioned an item. But when the buyer receives it, he or she is not satisfied. The seller offers a cheerful refund. However, what he or she gets back is a mess that doesn't much resemble the item he or she has shipped. Some buyers might attempt to swap out their junk for someone else's jewels.

PROTECTING AGAINST E-AUCTION FRAUD

The largest Internet auctioneer, eBay, has introduced several measures in an effort to reduce fraud. Some are free and some are not. The company has succeeded in its goal: only 27 out of every 1,000,000 transactions at eBay were fraudulent in 2000. Following are the measures they take:

USER IDENTITY VERIFICATION. EBay uses the services of Equifax to verify user identities for a $5 fee. Verified eBay User, the voluntary program, encourages users to supply eBay with information for online verification. By offering their social security number, driver's license number, and date of birth, users can qualify for the highest level of verification on eBay.

AUTHENTICATION SERVICE. Product authentication is a way of determining whether an item is genuine and described appropriately. Authentication is very difficult to perform because it relies on the expertise of the authenticators. Because of their training and experience, experts can often detect counterfeits based on subtle details (for a fee). However, two expert authenticators may have different opinions about the authenticity of the same item.

GRADING SERVICES. Grading is a way of determining the physical condition of an item, such as "poor quality" or "mint condition." The actual grading system depends on the type of item being graded. Different items have different grading systems—for example, trading cards are graded from A1 to F1, while coins are graded from poor to perfect uncirculated.

FEEDBACK FORUM. The eBay Feedback Forum allows registered buyers and sellers to build up their online trading reputations. It provides users with the ability to comment on their experiences with other individuals.

INSURANCE POLICY. EBay offers insurance underwritten by Lloyd's of London. Users are covered up to $200, with a $25 deductible. The program is provided at no cost to eBay users.

ESCROW SERVICES. For items valued at more than $200, or when either a buyer or seller feels the need for additional security, eBay recommends escrow services (for a fee). With an easy to access link to a third-party escrow service, both partners in a deal are protected.

The buyer mails the payment to the escrow service, which verifies the payment and alerts the seller when everything checks out. At that point, the seller ships the goods to the buyer. After an agreed-upon inspection period, the buyer notifies the service, which sends a check to the seller. (An example of a provider of online escrow services is i-Escrow.)

NON-PAYMENT PUNISHMENT. EBay implemented a policy against those who do not honor their winning bids. To help protect sellers, a first-time nonpayment results in a friendly warning. A sterner warning is issued for a second-time offense, with a 30-day suspension for a third offense, and indefinite suspension for a fourth offense.

APPRAISAL SERVICES. Appraisers use a variety of methods to appraise items, including expert assessment of authenticity and condition, and reviewing what comparable items have sold for in the marketplace in recent months. An appraised value is usually accurate at the time of appraisal but may change over time as an item becomes more or less popular in the marketplace.

VERIFICATION. Verification is a way of confirming the identity and evaluating the condition of an item. Third parties will evaluate and identify an item through a variety of means. For example, some collectors have their item "DNA tagged" for identification purposes. This provides a way of tracking an item if it changes ownership in the future.

2.9 Bartering Online

Bartering is the oldest method of trade. It is an exchange of goods and services, and today it is usually done between organizations. The problem in bartering is that it is difficult to find partners. Therefore, **bartering exchanges** were created, in which an intermediary arranges the transactions. The process works like this:

1. You tell the intermediary what you offer.
2. The intermediary assesses the value of your surplus products or services and offers you certain "points" (or "bartering dollars").
3. You use the "points" to buy the things you need.

The problem with manual matching done by a third party is that the commission is very high (30 percent or more), and it may take a long time to complete a transaction.

Electronic bartering **(e-bartering)** can improve the matching process by attracting more customers to the exchange. Also, the matching can be done faster. As a result, better matches can be found and the commission is much lower (5 to 10 percent).

Items that are frequently bartered include office space, storage, factory space, idle facilities and labor, products, and banner ads.

Businesses and individuals may use e-classified ads to advertise what they need and what they offer. However, exchanges can be much more effective. E-bartering may have tax implications that need to be considered. Some of the bartering Web sites are Bigvine.com, Bartertrust.com, ubarter.com, and lassoBucks.com (see Lorek, 2000).

Bartering sites must be financially secure. Otherwise users may not have a chance to use the points they accumulate. (For further details, see fsb.com, and search for "virtual bartering 101".)

As an alternative to bartering, you can auction your surplus and then use the money collected to buy what you need. Several auction sites specialize in surplus sales (e.g., tradeout.com).

2.10 Negotiating and Bargaining Online

Dynamic prices can also be determined by negotiation, especially for expensive or specialized products. It is a well-known process in the offline world, in real estate, automobiles, and agricultural products.

Much like auctions, negotiated prices result from interactions and bargaining among sellers and buyers. However, in contrast with auctions, negotiations also deal with non-pricing terms, such as payment method and credit.

According to Choi and Whinston (2000), negotiating in the electronic environment is easier than in the physical environment. Also, due to customization and bundling of products and services, it is necessary to negotiate prices and terms. E-markets allow negotiations to be used for virtually all products and services. Three factors may facilitate negotiated prices:

1. Intelligent agents that perform searches and comparisons, thereby providing quality customer service and a base from which prices can be negotiated.
2. Computer technology that facilitates the negotiation process.
3. Products and services that are bundled and customized.

One price does not fit all consumers, which sometimes makes price comparisons provided by MySimon and other online comparison-shopping services, difficult to execute, if not impossible. In personal services or insurance markets, because goods and services differ from individual to individual, we observe no posted prices that are easily identified. To the extent that there is no standard product to speak of at a standard price, digital products and services can be personalized as well as "integrated" as a smart service. Preferences for these bundled services differ among consumers, and thus they are combinations of services and corresponding prices.

TECHNOLOGIES FOR BARGAINING

According to Choi and Whinston (2000), negotiations and bargaining involve a bilateral interaction between a seller and a buyer who are engaged in the following five-step process that is necessary to complete a transaction:

- **Search.** Gathering information about products and services, locating potential vendors or customers.
- **Selection.** Processing and filtering information in order to select a product and a trading partner.
- **Negotiation.** Interactions with bids and offers, agreement, and contract.
- **Continuing Selection and Negotiation.** Repeated sequentially, if necessary, until an agreement is reached.
- **Transaction Completion.** Payment and delivery.

Search

Bargaining starts with collecting all relevant information about products and sellers or buyers. Computer-mediated markets excel in raising the search efficiency. Once information has been gathered, the next step is to process it into a usable data set that is employed for decision making.

Selection

Selection filters retrieve screened information that helps determine what to buy (sell) and from whom to buy (sell). This encompasses the evaluation of product and seller alternatives based on consumer-provided criteria such as price, warranty, availability, delivery time, and reputation. The selection process results in a set of names of products and partners to negotiate with in the next step. Software agents, such as **Personalogic.com**, and other tools can facilitate the selection.

Negotiation

The negotiation stage focuses on how to establish the terms of transaction, such as price, product characteristics, delivery, and payment terms. Negotiation varies in duration and complexity depending on the market. In online markets, all stages of negotiation can be carried out by automated programs or software agents.

Negotiation agents are software programs that make independent decisions to accept or reject offers or make bids within predetermined constraints. There might be negotiation rules or protocols by which agents of sellers and buyers interact. For example, price negotiation may start with a seller's list price as a starting point or in a free form starting with any bid or offer depending on the rule. (For an overview of electronic negotiation and comparison, see Beam et al. 2000.)

The following are the major benefits of electronic negotiations:

1. Buyers and sellers do not need to determine prices beforehand, and thereby do not have to engage in the difficult process of collecting relevant information. Negotiating prices transfers the burden of determining prices (i.e., market valuation) to the market itself. Insofar as the market process is efficient, the resulting negotiated prices will be fair and efficient.

2. Intelligent agents can negotiate both price and non-price attributes such as delivery time, return policy, and other value-added transactions. Intelligent agents can deal with multiple partners. An example of such an application is several freight dispatch centers of different companies negotiating a solution to their vehicle routing problems. Other applications include a factory floor-scheduling domain, where different companies in a subcontracting web negotiate over a joint scheduling problem, as well as an airport resource management domain, where negotiations take place for the servicing of airplanes between flights. (For further discussion, see Esmahi and Bernard 2000.)

Transaction Completion

After product, vendor, and price are determined, the final step is to complete the transaction. This involves online payment and product delivery in accordance with the terms determined in the negotiation phase. Other characteristics, such as customer service, warranty, and refunds, may also be implemented.

2.11 Mobile Auctions and the Future of Auctions

Research institutions have estimated that there will be 1.4 billion mobile phone users in the world by 2003, 50 percent of which will be Internet and Wireless Application Protocol (WAP) enabled. The mobile phone and other wireless devices are going to be the principal way for many people to come to the Internet, resulting in large volume m-commerce (Mobile Commerce). This opportunity is moving to auctions as well.

In the United States, eBay went wireless Internet in October 1999, and uBid and FairMarket started in 2000. Yahoo and other auction sites have been scrambling to go wireless. In the United Kingdom, **bluecycle.com**, which conducts auctions on used cars for dealers, allows dealers to bid from anywhere by using their cell phones.

There are some benefits and limitations of WAP phones for online auctions. Benefits include the following:

- **Convenience and Ubiquity.** People can do auction business on the go and from any location via mobile phone.
- **Privacy.** The WAP phone is more private than a PC and will always be within range. One can auction anything from anywhere and search for information in the middle of a discussion around the café table. Bids can be checked on the run. All this can transpire in a secure and private environment.
- **Simpler and Faster.** Because online auctions require a limited amount of information, it is relatively easy to adapt WAP-enabled phones, even if they can handle limited bandwidth and data.

Limitations include the following:

- **Visual Quality.** The WAP screen is very small. One cannot read through the same amount of information as on a computer. Also, the screen quality is not as good as on a PC monitor. One can send pictures of desired products to bidders via WAP, but if images are too complicated they will appear as blurs. It is also much harder to send information about products via the phone than via a PC.
- **Memory Capacity.** WAP phones have little memory capacity. In the near future, the development of new WAP services will probably press hardware producers to come up with better memory systems for mobile terminals.

- **Security.** The security issues particular to WAP are being tackled through new security standards, such as SIM Toolkit and wireless transport layer security.

GLOBAL AUCTIONS

Many auction companies sell products and services on the Web and are extending their reach. One way of doing that is by going global. However, such companies may face all the regular problems of selling online in foreign countries.

SELLING ART ONLINE IN REAL-TIME AUCTIONS

Since January 2001, collectors in the United Kingdom can bid online in live showroom auctions using an application of eBay and **icollector.com**. Icollector provides real-time access to 300 independent auction houses, such as London's Phillips. The largest art auction houses, Sotheby's and Christie's, have online sites, but they do not allow (as of spring 2001) online bidding for live showroom auctions. In the United States, **Butterfields.com** allows for real-time auction bidding and partners with eBay (see *New York Times*, January 22, 2001).

STRATEGIC ALLIANCES

Auctions may have a major impact on competition and on industry structure. In addition, auctions may be used as a strategic tool by Internet-based and other companies. An example for such strategy is provided in Application Case 2.4. It seems this type of strategic alliance will be very popular in the future due to its win-win possibilities.

2.12 Managerial Issues

YOUR OWN AUCTION SITE VS. A THIRD-PARTY SITE. This is a strategic issue, and there are pluses and minuses to each alternative. However, if you decide to auction from your site, you will need to advertise and attract visitors, which may be expensive. Also, you will need to install fraud-prevention mechanisms and provide services. Either way,

---

APPLICATION CASE 2.4

SOLD of Australia

SOLD (**sold.com.au**) is pioneering the online marketplace, where classified advertising and sales merge with the auction process to create a dynamic, fast growing e-commerce community. It is Australia's biggest online auction site. SOLD is a partnership between two leaders in the Internet industry—Fairfax Interactive Network (**fxj.com.au**) and Auctions Universal (**auctions.com**).

On September 13, 1999, SOLD and CitySearch (**citysearch.com.au**) the most popular Australia online leisure and lifestyle guide, launched a B2C program that provides small to medium-sized businesses (SMEs) with a web-based sales channel. This program enabled SMEs to use Australia's leading auction site as an outlet to sell general stock lines, excess stock, and discounted items.

Auction Shop, a division of SOLD, is offering brand-new computer products from leading manufacturers, and top quality equipment and household appliances. The offers give online consumers the chance to snare heavily discounted prices with warranties for a greater range of

new products including both excess stock and special price promotions.

SOLD had over 75,000 registered members by the end of 2000 and has had 40,000 sales for merchandise worth over $6 million dollars in its first six months of operation. By late 2000, there were 140,000 auction items on the site in over 170 categories, such as collectibles and memorabilia, business goods, sporting equipment, household items, travel and/or accommodation, millennium event tickets and venues, computer products, and Olympic pins.

In late 2000, the listing was free. The commission fee was 3.5% of the final selling price.

SOLD's B2C service offers users Merchant Manager—an inventory management and bulk-loading software that greatly reduces item listing time, assists in inventory management and profit analysis, and also provides additional invaluable post-auction services. Merchant Manager allows up to 4,000 items to be listed on the site in 30 minutes.

you may need to consider connectivity to your back-office and logistics system. The following are several issues that need to be handled by management.

1. **Cost-Benefit Analysis.** A major strategic issue is whether you need to do auctions or not. Auctions do have risks, and in forward auctions you may create a channel conflict with your other distribution channels.
2. **Auction Strategies.** Selecting an auction mechanism, pricing, and bidding strategy can be very complex for sellers. These strategies determine the success of the auction and the ability to attract and retain visitors on the site.
3. **Support Services.** Auctions require support services. Decisions about how to provide them and to what extent to use business partners are critical to the success of repeated high-volume auctions.
4. **Payment.** An efficient payment mechanism is important for auctions, especially when the buyers or the sellers are individuals. Some innovative methods can solve the payment problem.
5. **Controlling What is Auctioned.** Both individuals and companies would like to auction everything. However, is it ethical or even legal to do it? Ask eBay, which is trying, for example, to clean up pornographic auctions by banning some items and directing some items into a "mature audiences" area. Another issue is pirated software, which is offered on about 2,000 auction sites worldwide. As a matter of fact, eBay was sued in 2000 by video-game manufacturers Nintendo, Sega, and Electronic Arts. (For further discussion, see Beato 2000.)
6. **Change Agent.** Auctions may change the manner in which companies sell their products. They may change the nature of competition in certain industries, as well as price and margin levels.
7. **Building Auctions Applications.** Quite a few vendors offer auction software (e.g., see fairmarket.com).

   The process of building auction applications is complex for two reasons:

   1. The number of features can be very large (see Section 2.5 and Figure 2.7).
   2. There may be a need to integrate auctions in the B2B case, with the office and legacy systems of participating companies (see Figure 2.8).

8. **Bartering.** Bartering can be an interesting strategy, especially for companies that need cash and have some surpluses. However, the valuation of what is bought or sold may be different, and the tax implications in some countries are not clear.

Summary

The completion of this update helps you in attaining the following learning objectives:

- **Define the various types of auctions and list their characteristics.** In *forward auctions*, bids from buyers are placed sequentially, either increasingly (English mode) or decreasingly (Dutch mode). In *reverse auctions* buyers place an RFQ and suppliers submit offers, in one or several rounds. In "name-your-own-price" auctions, buyers specify how much they are willing to pay for a product or service and an intermediary tries to find a supplier to fulfill the request.
- **Describe the processes of conducting forward and reverse auctions.** In a forward auction the seller places the item to be sold on the auction site, with a starting price and closing time. Potential buyers bid from their PCs. The highest bids are constantly shown. At the close, the highest bidder wins. In a reverse auction, a buyer requests quotes for a product or service. These usually come in sequentially and the lowest bids are constantly shown. Reverse auctions are usually fast. The lowest-price bidder wins.
- **Describe the benefits and limitations of auctions.** The major benefits for sellers are the ability to reach many buyers and to sell quickly. Also, sellers save the commissions they might otherwise pay to intermediaries. Buyers have a

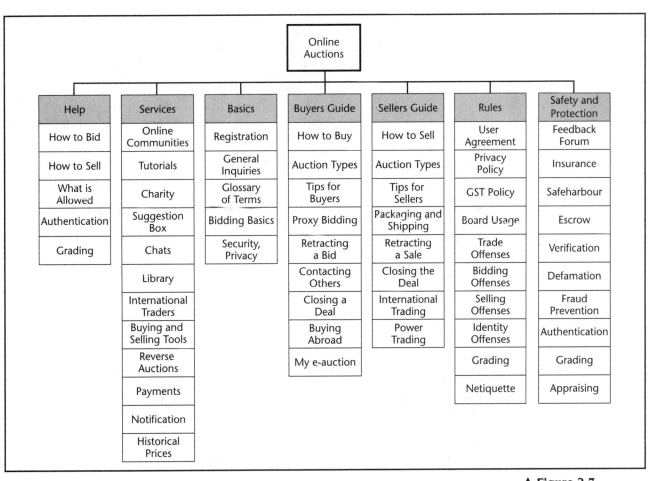

▲ Figure 2.7

Components of a Comprehensive Auction Site

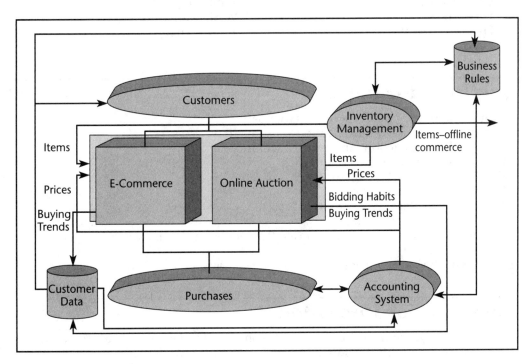

◄ Figure 2.8

Integrated Auction Business Model

chance to obtain collectibles while shopping from their homes, and they can find bargains. The major limitation is the possibility of fraud.

- **Describe the Various Services That Support Auctions.** Services exist along the entire process and include tools for (a) searching and comparing auctions for specific items, (b) registering, promoting, pricing, etc., (c) bid watching, making multiple bids, and proxy bidding, and (d) notification, payment, and shipping.
- **Describe the Hazards of e-auction Fraud and Countermeasures.** Fraud can be committed either by sellers or by buyers. Good auction sites provide protection that includes voluntary identity verification, monitoring of rules violation, escrow services, and insurance.
- **Describe Bartering and Negotiating.** Electronic bartering can greatly facilitate the swapping of goods and services among organizations, thanks to improved search and matching capabilities.
- **Analyze Future Directions and the Role of M-commerce.** B2B, C2C, G2B, and B2C auctions are all expanding rapidly. Future directions include an increase in global trading, use of wireless devices to monitor and trade at auctions, an increase in the use of intelligent agents in all steps, of the auction processes, and a merger of various types of auctions to allow traders more flexibility and choices.

Key Terms

Auction	Market maker
Auction vortals (vertical auctions)	"Name-your-own-price" model
Bartering	Negotiation online
Bartering exchanges	Proxy bidding
Double auction	Reserve price auction
Dutch auction	Reverse auction
Dynamic pricing	Single auction
E-auctions	Snipping
E-bartering	Stickiness
English auction	Tendering system
Forward auction	Vertical auction
Free-fall auction	Yankee auctions
Maximum bid	

Questions for Review

1. Define dynamic pricing and list its four parts.
2. Distinguish between forward and reverse auctions.
3. Define English auctions and Dutch auctions.
4. Describe the Priceline.com approach.
5. Define proxy bidding and describe its purpose.
6. What is meant by "snipping"?
7. List the advantages of e-bartering.
8. Define a double auction.
9. What are the benefits of e-auctions to the auction market makers?
10. Define a reserve price auction.
11. Describe the use of wireless technology in auctions.

Questions for Discussion

1. The "name-your-own-price" method is considered to be a reverse auction. There is no RFQ or consecutive bidding, so why is it called a reverse auction?

2. Discuss the advantages of dynamic pricing over fixed pricing. What are the potential disadvantages?
3. Find some material on why individuals like C2C auctions so much. Write a report.
4. Compare the "name-your-own-price" and RFQ approaches. Under what circumstances is each advantageous?
5. Identify three fraud practices in which a seller might engage. How can buyers protect themselves?
6. Identify three fraud practices in which a buyer might engage. How can sellers protect themselves?
7. It is said that Manheim Auction is trying to sell more online without cannibalizing its core business. Discuss this situation.
8. Discuss the need for software agents in auctions. Start by analyzing proxy bidding and auction aggregators.

Exercises

1. For each of the following situations, which (if any) dynamic pricing approach would you use and why?
   a. breeding and selling horses for racing
   b. buying flour for a bakery
   c. buying a horse for horse racing
   d. selling your used sport car, which is in high demand
   e. selling your old, obsolete PC system
   f. selling the stocks your grandfather left you as a gift
2. Enter **dellauction.com** and click on "site terms." Examine the policies, security and encryption statement, privacy protection statement, escrow services, payment options, and others. Register (for free), then bid on a computer of interest to you. If you are not interested, bid very low, so you will not get it.

   Alternatively, try to sell a computer. If you do not have one to sell, place an asking price so high that you will not get any bids. Read the FAQs. Which of the following mechanisms are used on the Dell site: English, Dutch (declining), reverse, etc. Why?

   Write a report on your experiences and describe all the features available at this site. *Note:* If you are outside the United States, use an auction site accessible from your location.
3. Compare **tradeout.com** and Yahoo!Auctions for selling surpluses. Use criteria such as fees paid by users, ease of use, execution, and mission. For more ideas about comparing sites, refer to *Interactiveweek*, September 13, 1999.
4. Imagine that you want to start forward auctions for a company with which you are familiar. Consider doing it in-house vs. using a third-party site. Write a comparative report.

Internet Exercises

1. Visit **eBay.com** and examine all the quality assurance measures available either for a fee or for free. Prepare a list.
2. Visit **AuctionWatch.com** and report on the various services offered at the site. What are the site's revenue models?
3. Enter **Bidfind.com** and report on the various services provided. What is the site's revenue model?
4. Enter **mmm.eBay.com** and investigate the use of "anywhere wireless." Review the wireless devices and find out how they work.
5. Enter **imandi.com** and review the process in which buyers can send RFQs to merchants of their choice. Also, evaluate the services provided in the areas of marketing, staffing, and travel. Write a report.

6. Examine the process used by office.com regarding auctions. Review its reverse auction arrangement with BigBuyer.com. Write a report.
7. Enter commerceone.com/auctions/iw3 and view all the different types of auction software and auction hosting available. Find what they have for a company-centric auction and learn about exchanges.
8. Enter iescrow.com and view the tutorial on how escrow services work for both buyers and sellers in electronic commerce.
9. Enter biddersedge.com and find historical prices on an item of your choice. How may this information be of help to you as a seller? As a buyer?
10. Enter respond.com and send a request for a product or a service. Once you receive replies, select the best deal. You have no obligation to buy. Write a short report on your experience.
11. Enter icollector.com and review the process used to auction art. Find support services, such as currency conversion and shipping. Take the tour of the site. Prepare a report on online buying as a collector.
12. Enter ubid.com and examine the "auction exchange." What is unique about it? Compare the auction there to those conducted on egghead.com. What are the major differences?

Team Assignments and Role Playing

1. Each item is assigned to an auction method (English, Dutch, etc.). Each team should convince a company that wants to liquidate items, that their method is the best. Items to be liquidated:
   a. Five IBM top line mainframe systems valued at about $500,000 each
   b. 750 PCs valued at about $1,000 each
   c. A real estate property valued at about $10 million.
   Present arguments for each type of item.
2. Assign teams to major auction sites from your country and from two other countries. Each team should present the major functionalities of the sites and the fraud protection measures they use.

REAL WORLD CASE: *FreeMarkets.com*

FreeMarkets.com began in 1995 with an idea: By conducting auctions online, procurement professionals could raise the quality of the direct materials and services they buy while substantially lowering the prices they pay for them.

FreeMarkets is a leader in creating B2B online auctions for buyers of industrial parts, raw materials, commodities, and services around the globe. The company created auctions for goods and services in more than 70 industrial product categories. In 1999, FreeMarkets auctioned more than $2.7 billion worth of purchase orders and saved buyers an estimated 2 to 25 percent.

FreeMarkets has helped customers source billions of dollars worth of goods and services in hundreds of product and service categories through its B2B Global Marketplace. FreeMarkets has also helped companies improve their asset recovery results by getting timely market prices for surplus assets through the FreeMarkets Asset Exchange.

FreeMarkets Asset Exchange creates a robust asset recovery solution that addresses even the most complex transactions. It bridges the gaps in information, geography, and industry that make traditional surplus-asset markets so inefficient.

FreeMarkets Asset Exchange provides a reliable, flexible trading platform that includes an online marketplace, online markets, and onsite auctions. With a combination of online and onsite sales venues, FreeMarkets Asset Exchange has the following solutions to help companies meet their asset recovery goals:

- **FreeMarkets Online Markets.** An effective method for asset disposal that delivers timely, market-based pricing.
- **FreeMarkets Online Marketplace.** A self-service venue where sellers post available assets. Useful when getting the right price is more important than a quick sale.
- **FreeMarkets Onsite Auctions.** Live auction events that are ideal for clearing a facility, time-critical sales, or selling a mix of high- and low-value assets.

When the commercial situation demands, the company also combines onsite auctions and online markets into a single asset disposal solution.

FreeMarkets Onsite Auctions provide the following:

- **Asset Disposal Analysis.** Market makers work with sellers to determine the best strategy to meet asset recovery goals.
- **Detailed Sales Offering.** The company collects and consolidates asset information into a printed or online sales offering for buyers.
- **Targeted Market Outreach.** FreeMarkets conducts targeted marketing to a global database of 500,000 buyers and suppliers.
- **Event Coordination.** The company prepares the site, provides qualified personnel, and enforces auction rules.
- **Sales Implementation.** FreeMarkets summarizes auction results and assists in closing sales.

Following is a customer's success story:

Emerson Corp., a global diversified manufacturing firm, faced the difficult challenge of consolidating millions of dollars of printed circuit board (PCB) purchases across 14 global divisions. The company wanted to consolidate its supply base and standardize data to understand future buying patterns. It turned to FreeMarkets for assistance.

Using RFQ, Emerson received 755 bids and achieved the following:

- Obtained buy-in from 14 divisions to participate in a corporate-wide event.
- Standardized data on more than 1,000 PCB designs across 19 divisions.
- Introduced several qualified suppliers from Asian countries.
- Consolidated its supplier's base from 58 to 9.

The company saved more than $10 million in 1 year.

Case Questions

1. Enter **FreeMarkets.com** and explore the current activities of the company.
2. Look at five customers' success stories. What common elements can you find?
3. Identify additional services provided by the company.
4. If you work in a company, register and examine the process as a buyer and as a seller.
5. Compare the use of **FreeMarkets.com** to the option of building your own auction site.
6. What is the logic of concentrating on asset recovery?
7. How does the surplus asset recovery become more efficient with FreeMarket?

References and Bibliography

Aberdeen Group (aberdeen.com), "The Moment: Providing Pricing Flexibility for eMarkets" (Boston, Mass: The Aberdeen Group, Inc., July 27, 2000).

Anonymous, "The Dynamic Pricing Revolution," at www.opensite.com/dcommerce/reference.asp.

C. Beam et al., "On Negotiations and Deal Making in Electronic Markets," *Information Systems Frontiers,* vol. 1:3, 1999.

G. Beato, "Online Piracy's Mother Ship," *Business2.com,* December 12, 2000.

R. Boileau, *The ABCs of Collecting Online,* 3rd ed. (Grantsville, Mich.: Hobby House Press, 2000).

S.Y. Choi and A.B Whinston, *The Internet Economy: Technology and Practice,* (Austin TX: SmarteconPub., 2000).

A. C. Elliot, *Getting Started in Internet Auctions* (New York: John Wiley & Sons, 2000).

L. Esmahi and J. C. Bernard, "MIAMAP: A Virtual Marketplace for Intelligent Agents," Proceedings of the 33rd HICSS, Maui, Hawaii, January 2000.

L. Fickel, "Bid Business," *CIO WebBusiness Magazine,* June 1, 1999.

Keenanvision.com, *The Keenan Report #1* (San Francisco: Keenan Vision Inc., 1998).

S. Klein, "Introduction to Electronic Auctions," *Electronic Markets,* vol. 7:4, 1997.

L. Lorek, "Trade ya? E-Barter Thrives," *InteractiveWeek,* August 14, 2000.

P. G. Mckeown, and R. T. Watson, "Manheim Auctions," *Communications of the Association for Information Systems,* June 1999.

A. Millen-Portor, "E-auction Model Morphs to Meet Buyers' Need," *Purchasing,* June 15, 2000.

R. Miner, *Dynamic Trading* (Tucson: Dynamic Trading Group, 1999).

B. S. Neo, "The Implementation of an Electronic Market for Pig Trading in Singapore," *Journal of Strategic Information Systems,* December 1992.

New York Times, January 22, 2001.

D. L. Prince, *Auction This!: Your Complete Guide to the World of Online Auctions* (Roseville, Calif.: Prima Publishing, 1999).

M. Strobel, "On Auctions as the Negotiation Paradigm of Electronic Markets," *Electronic Markets,* vol. 10:1, 2000.

D. Taylor and S. M. Cooney, *The e-Auction Insider* (Berkeley, Calif.: Osborne-McGraw Hill, 2000).

Y. Vakrat and A. Seidman, "Implications of Bidders' Arrival Process on the Design of Online Auctions," Proceedings of the 33rd HICSS, Maui, Hawaii, January 2000.

J. C. Westland, "Ten Lessons that Internet Auction Markets Can Learn from Securities Market Automation," *Journal of Global Management,* January–March 2000.

Wharton University, *Dynamic Pricing: What Does It Mean*? ebizchronicle.com/wharton/19-digital future, October 18, 2000.

P. R. Wurman et al., "Flexible Double Auctions for e-Commerce: Theory and Implementation," *Decision Support Systems.* vol. 24, 1998.

Intrabusiness, E-government and More

Update 3

3.1 Business Intelligence Portal Speeds Product Research and Development (R&D) at Amway

Amway Inc. sells through thousands of independent agents all over the world more than 450 home, nutrition and wellness, and personal products. To be effective, the R&D department at Amway must develop new products in a streamlined and cost-efficient manner. The R&D department consists of 550 engineers, scientists, and quality assurance staff working on more than 1,000 projects at a time.

Fast and easy access to information about current products such as product specifications, formulas, design criteria, production schedules, costs, and sales trends is required for supporting the design activity. This was difficult in the past because the required data resided sometimes in 15 to 20 disparate repositories, such as in a data warehouse, and supply chain and accounting systems were in different departments. When scientists needed production or financial data, for instance, they had to request paper reports from each department, which could take days to be processed.

Amway developed a business intelligence and knowledge management portal, called Artemis, tailored to the R&D division. Artemis is a browser-based intranet application that enables R&D staff to quickly find the required information. It also includes features such as collaboration tools and a database for locating company experts. Using the Lotus search agent and full-text search engine technology, Artemis enables employees to pull data from disparate corporate sources and generate dynamic reports in response to user queries.

Artemis started with the goal of saving each R&D employee one hour per week. Structured product data from legacy systems is abstracted by Artemis and used for creating dynamic reports in response to users' search criteria. Time required to access information dropped from days to minutes or seconds, enabling fast what-if investigations needed by product developers.

Amway's development partner, MarchFIRST, suggested that Lotus Domino would best leverage existing resources such as the intranet and data warehouse. Domino's strong security features, easy integration with legacy systems, built-in intelligent agents, and a fast search engine, along with powerful knowledge management capabilities, were instrumental in making Artemis a success.

With a budget of less than $250,000, Amway's IT support group users worked with MarchFIRST to complete Artemis over three phases of 8 to 12 weeks each, going live in January 2000. The portal runs on Domino 5.0 (in 2000), on a fast, dedicated Windows NT server. Each night, Domino sends intelligent agents out to a Sybase data warehouse and builds or updates an information document for each Amway product stored in a Domino database. R&D staff do full-text searches against this database to locate products of interest, then Domino queries the data warehouse for details. The only non-Domino part of Artemis is an $800 Java utility, called PopChart Live, used to create the trend and pie charts within the final document the user sees.

Collaborative features of Artemis include a time accounting function for the R&D staff. Used to help calculate R&D tax credits, this system has a gated section in which managers can analyze big-picture R&D trends. The Artemis event-reporting database also tracks project content and status, which helps staff to locate colleagues with specific expertise. Domino's strong messaging alerts staffers via e-mail when their projects are updated.

After a staged rollout, all 550 R&D staffers now have access to the system. Initial user surveys indicated that 60 percent are saving 30 minutes or more per week. This is expected to rise as links to more information sources are added and users gain comfort with the system.

Sources: Compiled from Abbott, C., "At Amway, BI Portal Speeds Product R&D," DM *Review*, October 2000, and from amway.com.

3.2 Intrabusiness and Business-to-Employee (B2E) E-commerce

The opening case demonstrates to us the importance of the corporate intranet in providing an infrastructure for knowledge sharing, and the role of the corporate portal as the gateway to this knowledge. The system enables fast access to information, provides security, and was constructed at a reasonable cost. The system will save about an hour a week, per employee, which is roughly equivalent to 13 employees out of the 550, paying for the system in less than six months. The intranet/portal application is an example of intrabusiness e-commerce.

E-commerce is not only done between business partners, but also within an organization. Such activity is referred to as **intrabusiness EC** or in short **intrabusiness**. Intrabusiness can be done between the following:

- a business and its employees (B2E)
- among units within the business (usually done as c-commerce)
- among employees in the same business (usually done as c-commerce)

BUSINESS TO ITS EMPLOYEES (B2E)

Later in this Update we will show several examples of B2E. Here are some representative ones:

- Employees electronically order supplies and material needed for their work.
- Many companies have corporate stores that sell a company's products to its employees, usually at a discount. The employees place orders on the intranet, and the store will pack and deliver the items to the employees, at work or at home. Payment is then deducted from payroll.
- Businesses disseminate information on the intranet (section 3.4).
- Employees can buy discounted insurance, travel packages, and tickets to events on the corporate intranet.
- Businesses allow employees to manage their fringe benefits, take classes, and much more, all electronically (Sections 3.3, 3.4).

BETWEEN AND AMONG UNITS WITHIN THE BUSINESS

Large corporations frequently consist of independent units, or single business units (SBUs), which "sell" or "buy" materials, products, and services from each other. Transactions of this type can be easily automated and performed over the intranet. An SBU can be considered as either a seller or a buyer.

Large corporations also have a net of dealerships that are usually wholly or partially owned by the corporation. In such a case, a special network is constructed to support communication, collaboration, and execution of transactions. Such intrabusiness commerce is conducted by autodealers, equipment manufacturers (e.g., Caterpiller), and most other large manufacturers, including those dealing with consumer products such as in the case of Toshiba America (see Application Case 3.1).

BETWEEN AND AMONG CORPORATE EMPLOYEES

Many large organizations have classified ads on the intranet through which employees can buy and sell products and services from each other. This service is especially popular in universities where it has been conducted since even before the commercialization of the Internet. (Note that in some cases several universities interconnect their intranets to increase the exposure, such as in the case of the universities in Singapore.)

In addition, employees collaborate and communicate using EC technologies. The most popular infrastructure for intrabusiness is the *intranet*.

3.3   Intranets

An **intranet**, or an internal Web, is a network architecture designed to serve the internal informational needs of a company using Web concepts and tools. It provides Internet capabilities, namely easy and effective browsing, search engines, and a tool for communication and collaboration. Using a Web browser, a manager can see resumes of employees, business plans, and corporate regulations and procedures; retrieve sales data; review any desired document; and call a meeting. Employees can check availability of software for particular tasks and test the software from their workstations. Intranets are frequently connected to the Internet, enabling the company to conduct e-commerce activities, such as cooperating with suppliers and customers or checking a customer's inventory level before making shipments. Such activities are facilitated by *extranets*. Using screen sharing and other groupware tools, the intranets can be used to facilitate the work of groups. Companies also publish newsletters, deliver news to their employees, and conduct online training on their intranet. Some applications of intranet commerce are provided later.

The cost of converting an existing client-server network to an internal Web is relatively low, especially when a company is already using the Internet. Many computing facilities can be shared by both the Internet and intranets. An example is a client–server-based electronic conferencing software (from Picture Talk, Inc., **picturetalk.com**) that allows users to share documents, graphics, and video in real time. This capability can be combined with an electronic voice arrangement.

According to a Meta Group study (Stellin, 2001), nearly 90 percent of all U.S. corporations have some type of intranet, and over 25 percent are using corporate portals—sites

Intrabusiness E-commerce at Toshiba America

The Problem. Toshiba America has an intranet that doubles as a dealer extranet. Toshiba works with 300 dealers. Dealers who needed parts quickly had to place a telephone or fax order by 2:00 P.M. for next-day delivery. To handle the shipment, Toshiba's Electronic Imaging Division (EID) (fax machines and copiers) spent $1.3 million on communications and charged $25 per shipment to the dealers. In addition, dealers had to pay the overnight shipping fee. A cumbersome order-entry system was created in 1993, but no significant improvement was achieved.

The Solution. In August 1997, Toshiba created a Web-based order-entry system using an extranet/intranet. Dealers now can place orders for parts until 5:00 P.M. for next-day delivery. The company placed the physical warehouse in Memphis, Tennessee, near FedEx headquarters to ensure quick delivery. Dealers can also check accounts receivable balances and pricing arrangements, and read

service bulletins, press releases, and so on. Once orders are submitted, a computer checks for the part's availability. If a part is available, the order is sent to Toshiba's warehouse in Memphis. Once at the warehouse site, the order pops up on a handheld radio frequency (RF) monitor. Within a few hours the part is packed, verified, and packaged for FedEx. See Figure 3.1.

The intranet also allows sales reps to interact more effectively with dealers. The dealers can be up-to-date and manage their volume discount quotes up to the minute.

The Results. Using the system, the cost per order has declined to about $10. The networking cost of EID has been reduced by more than 50 percent (to $600,000/year). The low shipping cost results in 98 percent overnight delivery, which increases customer satisfaction. The site processes more than 85 percent of all dealers' orders.

For further details, see *CIO Web Magazine*, July 1, 1999.

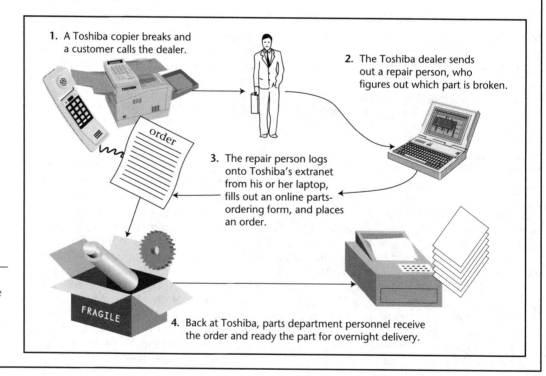

Figure 3.1

Toshiba's Customer Service Process

Source: Compiled from Jones (1998). Used by permission.

1. A Toshiba copier breaks and a customer calls the dealer.

2. The Toshiba dealer sends out a repair person, who figures out which part is broken.

3. The repair person logs onto Toshiba's extranet from his or her laptop, fills out an online parts-ordering form, and places an order.

4. Back at Toshiba, parts department personnel receive the order and ready the part for overnight delivery.

that perform functions well beyond publishing material on the intranet. Intranets, which received a lot of publicity in the 1990s, are back in the limelight as a growing number of organizations are now putting new energy into them.

Intranets are fairly safe, operating within the company's firewalls. Employees can venture out into the Internet, but unauthorized users cannot come in. This arrangement lets companies speed information and software safely to their own employees and business partners.

Wireless LANs Speed Hospital Insurance Payments

The Bridgeton, is a U.S. holding company that operates four hospitals in New Jersey. The company is using wireless LANs to process insurance documentation so that the number of claims denied by insurers can be reduced. Nurses log on to the network using their notebook computers to access the hospital's intranet, pharmacy, and labs and use e-mail.

The network environment broadcasts data over a distance of about 120 feet located above nursing workstations. Nurses can move from the station into patient rooms while maintaining a network connection. As a nurse takes a notebook computer from one nursing station to another, the radio card in the notebook computer goes into a roaming mode similar to a cellular phone. The company is getting a good return on investment, savings in six-figure dollar amounts, for a moderate cost of setting up the network (about $200 for each notebook computer radio card and $750 for each of 28 wireless access points).

Source: Compiled from Computerworld, April 10, 2000, p. 74.

Intranets change organizational structures and procedures and help reengineer corporations. Application Case 3.2 illustrates the example of a wireless local area network (LAN) and its benefits in accessing a hospital intranet and other applications.

Other examples include:

- In 2000, Financial Times (FT) Electronic Publishing implemented its online news and information service, FT Discovery, to 10,000 intranet users at KPMG. FT Discovery is integrated into the KPMG corporate intranet to provide immediate access to critical business intelligence from over 4,000 information sources. For example, corporate Navigator from Story Street Partners is integrated into the intranet to provide in-depth advice on where to go for information on the issues and companies of interest to KPMG.

  (*Source:* idm.internet.com/articles/200007/ic_07_26_00e.html, July 2000.)

- All the Hawaiian islands are linked by a state educational, medical, and other public services network (**htdc.org**). This ambitious intranet provides quality services to residents of all islands.

  (*Source:* htdc.org.)

- Employees at IBM ranked the intranet as the most useful and credible source of information. They use the intranet to order supplies, sign up for fringe benefits, take classes, track projects, and manage their retirement plans. IBM considers its intranet an extremely valuable source of information that helps to increase productivity. For example, managers can post and read information about projects in progress without bothering people, making calls, or sending e-mails. IBM employees who telecommute can log onto the intranet from home and conduct work. In May 2001, IBM called its employees to contribute ideas for solving current problems. More than 6,000 suggestions were collected in three days.

  (*Source:* Compiled from the *New York Times*, January 29, 2001.)

- At Charles Schwab, 25,000 employees use the intranet regularly. It helps employees provide better customer service, because it is much easier to respond to customers' inquiries. Using superb search engines employees can find the answers, by themselves, quickly and without asking other employees. It is a standard now to look at the intranet first, in order to find answers. Schwab estimates tens of millions of dollars in savings due to the intranet.

  (*Source:* Condensed from the *New York Times*, January 29, 2001.)

To build an intranet, we need Web servers, browsers, Web publishing tools, back-end databases, TCP/IP networks (LAN or WAN), and firewalls, as shown in Figure 3.2. A firewall is software and/or hardware that allows only those external users with specific char-

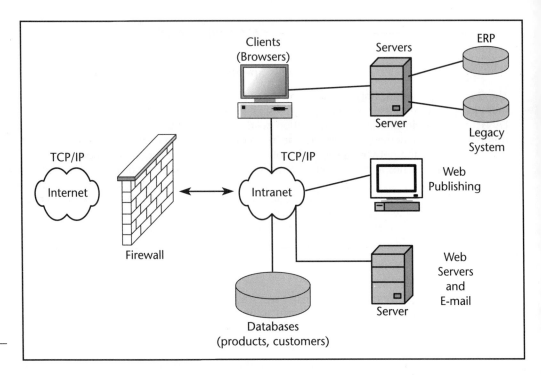

Figure 3.2

Architecture of Intranet

acteristics to access a protected network. Additional software may be necessary to support the Web-based workflow, groupware, and enterprise resource planning (ERP), depending upon the individual company's need. The security schemes for the intranet are basically the same as the ones for the Internet.

A company may have one intranet composed of many LANs. Alternatively, a company may have several interconnected intranets, each composed of only a few LANs. The decision of how to structure the intranet depends on how dispersed the LANs are, and what technologies are involved.

3.4   Intranets Functionalities and Applications

In this section, we review some intranet applications, but let's first look at the major functionalities of an intranet which can include corporate, department, and individual Web pages.

INTRANET FUNCTIONALITIES

Intranets have some or all of the following:

- Web-based database access for ease of use
- Search engines, indexing engines, and directories that assist keyword-based search
- Interactive communication such as chatting, audio support, and videoconferencing
- Document distribution and workflow including Web-based downloading and routing of documents
- Groupware including enhanced e-mail, bulletin board, screen sharing, and other group support tools
- Conduit for the computer-based telephony system

In addition, intranets usually have the capability to integrate with EC, interface with Internet-based electronic purchasing, payment, and delivery, and be part of extranets (geographically dispersed branches, customers, and suppliers can access certain portions of the intranets). These functions provide for numerous applications that increase productivity, reduce cost, reduce waste and cycle time, and improve customer service.

INTRANET APPLICATION AREAS AND BENEFITS

According to a survey conducted by *InformationWeek* with 988 responding managers (Chabrow, 1998), information that is most frequently included in intranets is in the form of product catalogs (49 percent of all companies), corporate policies and procedures (35 percent), purchase ordering (42 percent), document sharing (39 percent), corporate phone directories (40 percent), human resource forms (35 percent), training programs, customer databases, data warehouse and decision support access, image archives, purchase orders, enterprise suits, and travel reservation services. These figures are much higher today, since intranets are maturing.

In addition to the many activities listed, intranets also provide the following benefits:

- **Electronic commerce**: Intrabusiness marketing can be done online; selling to outsiders is done via the extranet, and it involves portions of the intranet.
- **Customer service**: UPS, FedEx, and other pioneering companies have proved that information about product shipments and availability make customers happier. Again, the intranet-extranet combination is used.
- **Search and access to documents:** The intranet provides access to any information that can increase productivity and facilitate teamwork.
- **Personalized information.** The intranet can deliver personalized information, via personalized Web pages and e-mail.
- **Enhanced knowledge sharing:** The Web-based intranet can enhance knowledge sharing.
- **Enhanced group decision and business processes**: Web-based groupware and workflow are becoming part of the standard intranet platform. These can be part of the internal supply chain operation.
- **Empowerment:** More employees can be empowered because they can easily access the right information and online expertise to make decisions.
- **Virtual organizations:** Web technology used by business partners removes the barrier of incompatible technology between businesses.
- **Software distribution:** Using the intranet server as the application warehouse helps to avoid many maintenance and support problems.
- **Document management:** Employees can access pictures, photos, charts, maps, and other documents regardless of where they are stored, and where the employees' work bases are located.
- **Project management:** Most project management activities are conducted over intranets.
- **Training:** The Web page is a valuable source of knowledge to novices.
- **Enhanced transaction processing:** Data can be entered efficiently through the intranet and only once, thus eliminating errors and increasing internal control.
- **Paperless information delivery**: Eliminating paper by disseminating information on the intranet can result in lower cost, easier accessibility, greater efficiency in maintenance, and better security.
- **Improved administrative processes**: The internal management of production, inventory, procurement, shipping, and distribution can be effectively supported by linking these functions in a single threaded environment—the intranet—and these functions can also be seamlessly integrated with the interorganizational extranets.

INDUSTRY-SPECIFIC INTRANET SOLUTIONS

Intranet solutions are frequently classified by industry instead of technology, because the technology is no longer a bottleneck for implementation. The development of business models has become a critical concern for the managerial success of intranets. According to the classification of *InformationWeek Online*, the top 100 intranet and extranet solutions can be classified by industry as follows (Solution Series, 1998): financial services (banking, brokerages and other financial services, and insurance), information technology, manufacturing (chemicals and oil, consumer goods, food and beverage, general manufacturing, and pharmaceuticals), retail, and services (construction/engineering, education, environmental, health care, media, entertainment, telecommunications, transportation, and utilities).

Internet applications are very diversified. Now, let us look at some typical applications in more depth, including their return on investment (ROI).

INTRANET CASE STUDIES

International Data Corporation (idc.com) compiled a collection of successful intranet case applications by world-class companies such as Amdahl Corporation; Booz, Allen & Hamilton; Cadence Design Systems Inc.; Deere & Company; Lockheed Martin Corporation; Silicon Graphics, Inc.; and Southern California Gas Company. New cases are being added periodically. Each case includes background of the company, business challenges, before-intranet technology, intranet cost, intranet strategy, after-intranet technology, subjective benefits (optional), lessons learned, and analysis of ROI. Older cases are available at netscape.com. The Cadence Design Systems Inc. case is summarized in the Real World Case at the end of this Update. Other representative's cases include the following:

Moen—Connected ERP.

Moen Corp. (North Olmstead, Ohio) launched an intranet called CinfoNet in 1997. Moen needed to share information quickly and easily, especially with a huge SAP R/3 system that was implemented at that time. The development team included three employees and several consultants. A favorite user application was the product database. Initially, 70 percent of Moen's 2,500 employees had access to the intranet. When R/3 was implemented, 100 percent were on the intranet. To make CinfoNet a complete success, existing electronic documents were converted to the new system.

Compaq Computer Corp.—Investment Assistant.

Compaq's employees use the intranet to access the company and to communicate from anywhere, but it has another unique feature. Staff members can also access the human resources database for such information as their retirement accounts. Employees can then choose to reallocate the investments that they have in the account; they have a great deal of latitude and control over their retirement plans and how they perform. This enables them to choose where their money goes and gives them individual responsiblility for the performance and growth of their funds. In addition, they can choose benefits, learn about training programs, and much more. Many other companies put such benefit programs on the intranet.

Silicon Graphics, Inc.—Share Huge Internal Web Sites.

Silicon Graphics makes high-end graphics workstations. Their intranet system, called Silicon Junction, is accessed by over 7,000 employees. It includes 800 specialized internal Web sites containing more than 144,000 pages of technical information. There is also access to all corporate databases, which was previously not possible. Information that once took days to access can now be obtained in a few minutes, simply by using links, pointing, and clicking.

Coopers & Lybrand: Share knowledge among corporate employees.

Coopers & Lybrand, one of the five largest CPA, taxation, and consulting firms, developed a special **knowledge curve intranet**. It originated as a service for company consultants and corporate tax professionals who handle taxes for *Fortune* 1,000 corporations. It was shifted to the Web in 1997. The knowledge curve is now integrated with the Tax News Network (TNN), an extranet for tax consultants for whom Coopers & Lybrand created a one-stop interactive information source on the constantly changing tax laws and regulations. The network contains tax information from numerous sources, integrating internal and external and even competing resources. In addition, it includes full text of various tax analyses, legislative tax codes, and major business newspapers. It is available to 75,000 employees and consultants of Coopers & Lybrand worldwide who use Lotus Notes Domino as a standard communications and collaboration system.

The company combined a series of automated Notes and third-party applications, to replicate internal documents that are published on TNN, across company Notes servers. Company researchers can post their tax findings within Notes bulletin boards and set up database replication systems in Notes, which can be transformed into separate Notes databases on the extranet. The TNN extranet requires potential members to register and receive a password. The extranet runs on three servers located at the Information Access Company data center in Medford, Massachusetts, where backbone communications facilities are particularly suitable for efficient worldwide transmission. This is an example of a corporate knowledge base deliverable on an intranet and extranet. A similar system is available at Arthur Andersen for their knowledgespace.com. (For knowledge base application, see Internet Exercise 7 at the end of this Update.)

Corporate intranets are infrastructures that enable many Web-based applications and they are usually accessed via the corporate portal.

3.5   Enterprise (Corporate) Portals

With growing use of intranets and the Internet, many organizations encounter difficulties in dealing with information overload at different levels. Information is scattered across numerous documents, e-mail messages, and databases at different locations and systems. Finding relevant and accurate information is often time consuming and requires access to multiple systems.

As a consequence, organizations and their employees lose a lot of productive time. One solution is to use portals. Kounadis (2000) defines a **corporate (enterprise) portal** as a personalized, single point of access through a Web browser to critical business information located inside and outside of an organization. A portal is a gateway and a corporate portal is a gateway to corporate information. It attempts to address information overload through an intranet-based environment to search and access relevant information from disparate IT systems and the Internet, using advanced search and indexing techniques.

Portals appear under many descriptions and shapes. One way to distinguish among them is to look at their content, which can vary from narrow to broad, and their community, or audience, which can also vary widely. When combined, one can create a matrix of portals as shown in Figure 3.3.

According to this matrix we distinguish four types of portals:

Figure 3.3

Types of Portals

1. *Publishing portals* are intended for large and diverse communities with diverse interests. These portals involve relatively little customization of content except online search and some interactive capabilities, which would be typical for the Web. (Examples are techweb.com or zdnet.com.)
2. *Commercial portals* offer narrow content for diverse communities and are the most popular portals today for the online communities. Although they offer customization of the user's interface, they are still intended for broad audiences and offer fairly simple content (a stock ticker, news on a few preselected items). Examples are My Yahoo! and Excite.

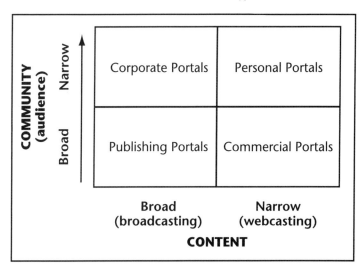

3. *Personal portals* target specific filtered information for individuals. As with commercial portals, they offer relatively narrow content but are typically much more personalized with an effective audience of one.

4. *Corporate portals* coordinate rich content within a relatively narrow community. They are also known as enterprise portals, or enterprise information portals. These are portals built with large enterprise intranet applications. The portal content is much broader than that of a commercial portal, because of the greater diversity of information used to make decisions in an organization. Specifically, a corporate portal offers a single point of entry, which brings together the employees, business partners, and consumers at one virtual place. Through the portal, these people can create structured and personalized access to information across large, multiple, and disparate enterprise information systems, as well as the Internet. A schematic view of a corporate portal is provided in Figure 3.4.

In contrast with publishing and commercial portals, such as Yahoo!, which are only a gateway to the Internet, corporate portals provide single-point access to the information and applications available on the Internet, intranets, and extranets. Corporate portals are an extended form of intranets that offer employees and customers an organized focal point for their interactions with the firm.

Many large organizations are already implementing portals to cut costs, free up time for busy executives and managers, and add to the bottom line (*Informationweek.com,* May 2000). Corporate portals are popular in large corporations, as shown in Application Case 3.3 on page 58.

According to a Delphi Group's survey (see *Datamation,* July 1999), over 55 percent of the 800 respondents have already begun corporate portal projects with about 42 percent of these conducting the projects at the enterprise level. The top portal applications, in decreasing order of importance, found from their survey are as follows:

- Knowledge bases and learning tools
- Business process support
- Customer-facing sales, marketing, and services
- Collaboration and project support
- Access to data from disparate corporate systems

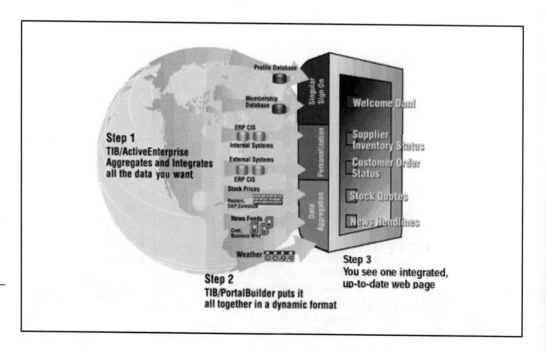

Figure 3.4

Corporate Portal as Gateway to Information

Source: Tibco.com

- Personalized pages for users
- Effective search and indexing tools
- Internal company information
- High level of security
- Policies and procedures
- Best practices and lessons learned
- Human resources and benefits
- Directories and bulletin boards
- Identification of experts
- News and Internet

The Delphi Group also found that poor organization of information and lack of navigation and retrieval tools contribute to over 50 percent of the problems for corporate portal users. For further details see **delphigroup.com/pubs/corporate-portal-excerpt.htm.**

Figure 3.5 depicts a corporate portal framework based on Aneja et al. (2000) and Kounadis (2000). This framework illustrates the features and capabilities required to support various organizational activities using internal and external information sources. For guidelines to define corporate portal strategy, see Table 3.1.

Figure 3.5

Corporate Portal Framework

Compiled by N. Bolloju, City University of Hong kong rom Anbefa et al. 2000 and from Kounadis 2000.

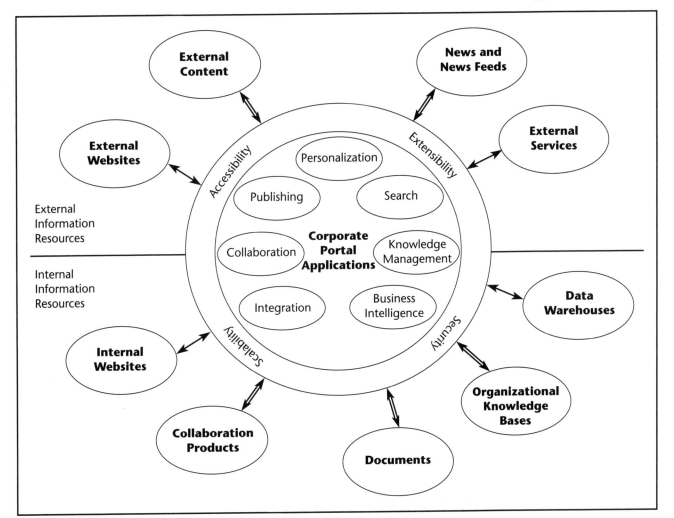

Corporate Portals at Procter & Gamble, DuPont, and Staples

Procter & Gamble's IT division developed a system for sharing documents and information over the company's intranet. The scope of this system has expanded into a global knowledge catalogue to support the information needs of all 97,000 P&G employees worldwide. Although the system helped in providing required information, it also led to information overload. To solve this problem, P&G developed a corporate portal that provides personalized information to each employee that can be accessed through a Web browser without the need to navigate through 14 different Web sites. P&G's corporate portal, implemented by Plumtree (**plumtree.com**), provides P&G's employees with marketing, product and strategic information, and industry-news documents, numbering over one million Web pages, in thousands of Lotus Notes databases. Employees can gain access to the required information through customized preset views of various information sources and links to other up-to-date information.

DuPont & Co. began implementing an internal portal to organize millions of pages of scientific information stored in information systems throughout the company.

The initial version of the portal was intended for daily use by over 550 employees to record product orders, retrieve progress reports for research products, and access customer-tracking information. DuPont plans to extend the portal to between 20,000 to 60,000 employees in 30 business units in various countries.

Staples' corporate portal, launched in February 2000, is used by 3,000 executives, knowledge workers, and store managers. Staples is expecting that the portal will grow to support 10,000 of the 46,000 employees and serve as the interface to business processes and applications. The portal is used by top management, as well as by managers of contracts, procurement, sales and marketing, human resources, and the retail store. It is also used for internal business by Staples' three business-to-business Web sites. The portal offers e-mail, scheduling, headlines on the competition, new product information, internal news, job postings, and newsletters.

Sources: Compiled from *Informationweek* May 1, 2000, and from staples.com

Table 3.1

Key Steps to Corporate Portal Strategy

- Identify the content that is or will be available, and identify where this content resides.
- Leverage existing systems, resources, and repositories.
- Include both structured and unstructured information.
- Organize content into categories that can be browsed and searched.
- Integrate search functionality across multiple information repositories.
- Build a platform for publishing and subscribing to content.
- Deliver personalized content and services to users based on their performances and roles.
- Develop the corporate portal in phases.
- Create online communities to connect people and enable collaborative work.
- Develop an extensible architecture that allows for extended functionality.
- Sustain a collaborative portal by institutionalizing it within daily business operations and weaving it into long-term strategies.
- Purchase an integrated portal product rather than building custom portal functionality.

Source: Compiled from Aneja et al. Corporate Portal Framework for Transforming Content Chaos on Intranets, *Intel Technology Journal*, Q1, 2000.

3.6 Example of an Intranet and a Portal: Cadence Design Systems

Cadence Design Systems Inc. is a leading supplier of electronic design automation (EDA) software tools and professional services for managing and accelerating the design of semiconductors, computer systems, networking and telecommunications equipment, consumer electronics, and other electronic-based products. The San Jose–based company employs more than 3,000 people in offices worldwide to support the development requirements of the world's leading electronic manufacturers.

BUSINESS CHALLENGE

Early in 1995, Cadence recognized that the business model for EDA products was beginning to evolve from a tools orientation to one where the value placed on software and consulting services held the potential for the greatest revenue growth. Rather than sell a single product, Cadence wanted to support the customer's entire product development cycle.

To understand and address this changing model, Cadence identified two areas of customer interaction: sales and delivery. The new sales strategy required the sales force to have an in-depth understanding of Cadence's product line of almost 1,000 products and services. With two separate organizations interacting with customers, coordination and communication were needed to ensure an effective and consistent relationship built on a real understanding of the customer's issues.

THE SOLUTION: INTRANET AND PORTAL TECHNOLOGY

For almost a year, Cadence worked with a consulting firm to create a corporate portal—a Web-based single point of information, for supporting the sales organization. This system, called OnTrack, uses a home page with links to other pages, information sources, and custom applications to map each phase of the sales process with supporting materials and reference information. By adopting OnTrack, Cadence achieved the high return on investment of 1,766 percent.

With OnTrack, the sales rep now has a single unified tool that provides all information and data needed to go through the sales process from prospecting to closing a deal and account management. In addition, global account teams have their own home page where they can collaborate and share information. However, OnTrack is more than a static road map. A sales rep can initiate workflow automatically, eliminating the hurdle of needing to know who to call. Information on a customer or competitor is now available instantly through access to an outside provider of custom news. The sales rep can simply search, using a company name, to get everything from financial information to recent news articles and press releases.

All creators of information in the company, from sales reps to marketing and management personnel, are responsible for maintaining the information contained in OnTrack. With a wide range of people entering data, a simple-to-use information submission process was needed. To avoid the need to understand HTML, forms were created to allow submission or modification of any part of the information in the OnTrack system. Anyone with appropriate access can now add a new message to the daily alerts, modify a step in the sales process, or update a customer presentation by using these custom tools. Feedback is also a key part of OnTrack. Reports highlight frequently accessed pages and documents, and reviews of frequent searches look to include new information and make critical information easier to access.

LESSONS LEARNED

Those who adopted the OnTrack learned several lessons. First, balancing the cost of training against the return is a difficult task. Although the use of a browser and the navigation of a Web page required minimal training, the application of the OnTrack system to the daily activities of a sales rep was not easy. OnTrack supported a reengineering of the sales process, and Cadence believed that demonstrating the use of OnTrack in supporting the sales rep might have accelerated the use of the system.

Second, for Cadence, the key to success was the holistic approach taken to unifying the technology with the process. Rather than mandate a new process, or install a new software system, the combination of an easy-to-use technology, a refined process, and the appropriate personnel and support systems created a single coherent system that could support the new sales paradigm.

Cadence also worked to design a process and infrastructure that could satisfy 80 percent rather than 100 percent of the sales situations. This strategy helped the company in two ways: (1) It is often more effective to refine a system after gaining experience than to attempt to design the perfect system from the beginning, and (2) a process that can address all possible exceptions is often an exercise in futility. One reason Cadence has achieved such a high return on investment is its focus on supporting the bulk of work process rather than the entire process.

A relatively low cost was needed to implement OnTrack. Cadence leveraged its existing infrastructure and wisely hired outside experts to create the application rather than devoting internal resources. This choice allowed the company to focus its efforts on defining the process and tools needed to support the sales force rather than designing software.

Lastly, the greatest impact is the result of the shortened training time for new sales reps. A new salesperson stated that he had learned in 2 days from OnTrack what it took months to learn at a previous company. With 40 new reps hired in the first year, and 40 planned for each of the next 2 years, reducing the training time for new sales personnel had a substantial impact on additional profits to Cadence.

Collaborative Commerce.

Collaborative commerce **(C-commerce)** is when employees from different organizations design, plan, communicate, and implement projects together on the Web. The same applies to intrabusiness collaboration, where employees of different units collaborate using the intranets and corporate portals.

3.7 E-government: An Overview

As e-commerce matures and its tools and applications improve, greater attention is given to its use to improve the business of public institutions and governments (country, state, county, city etc). Several international conferences were organized in 2000 and 2001 to explore the potential of what is called e-government. **E-government** is the use of information technology in general, and e-commerce in particular, to provide citizens and organizations with more convenient access to government information and services; and to provide delivery of public services to citizens, business partners and suppliers, and those working in the public sector. It is also an efficient and effective way of conducting business transactions with citizens and other businesses and within the governments themselves.

Definitions.

- E-government is an opportunity to improve the efficiency and effectiveness of the executive functions of government including the delivery of public services. It also enables governments to be more transparent to citizens and businesses by providing access to more of the information generated by government.
- E-government facilitates fundamental changes in the relationships between the citizens and the state, and between nation states, with implications for the democratic process and structures of government (UK government).
- E-government is a way for governments to use Internet technologies to provide people with more convenient access to government information and services, to improve the quality of the services, and to provide greater opportunities to participate in our democratic institutions and processes (New Zealand Government).
- E-government in the U.S. was especially driven by the 1998 Government Paperwork Elimination ACT and by President Clinton December 17, and by the 1999 Memorandum of e-government that ordered the top 500 forms used by citizens to be placed on line by December 2000. The Memorandum also directed agencies to construct a secure e-government infrastructure.
- E-government is the application of information technology to the processes of government. It has been defined as digital information and online transaction

services to citizens. Others use the term as an extension of e-commerce to government procurement and see it only in the realm of B2G (business to government) transactions.

(*Source:* International Trade Center-Executive Forum 2000 intracen.org/execforum/docs/ef2000/eb200010.htm).

- E-government is the birth of a new market and the advent of a new form of government—a form of government that is a powerful force in the Internet economy, bringing together citizens and businesses in a network of information, knowledge, and commerce.

3.8 Major Categories of Applications of E-government

GOVERNMENT-TO-CITIZENS

In the **government-to-citizen (G2C)** category, we include all the interactions between a government and its citizens. As shown in this Update's Real World Case in Hong Kong, G2C involves dozens of different initiatives. The basic idea is to allow citizens to interact with the government from their homes. Citizens can find all the information they need on the Web, can ask questions and receive answers, pay tax and bills, receive payments and documents, and so forth. Governments disseminate information on the Web, conduct training, help in finding employment, and more. In California, for example, drivers' education classes are offered online, and can be taken at any time, from anywhere. As a matter of fact, government agencies and departments in many cities, counties, and countries are planning more and more diverse e-services. For example, many governments are now seriously considering electronic voting. In some countries, voters actually see their choice on the computer screen and are asked to confirm their vote, much as is done when purchasing a book from Amazon, transferring funds, or selling stocks (see Schwartz, 2000 for further discussion on this topic).

Electronic Benefits Transfer (EBT).

The United States transfers more than $500 billion in benefits annually to its citizens. More than 20 percent of these transfers go to citizens who do not have bank accounts. In 1993, the U.S. government launched an initiative to develop a nationwide electronic benefits transfer (EBT) system to deliver government benefits electronically. This approach relies upon a single smart card, to access cash and food benefits at automated teller machines and point-of-sale locations, just like other bank card users do with their smart cards. EBT brings users convenience and dignity, dramatically reducing theft, fraud, and abuse of benefits. Also, the cost of dispensing benefits electronically is much lower.

The federal EC program is implementing a nationwide EBT system. Agencies at the federal, state, and local levels are expanding EBT programs into new areas, including health, nutrition, employment, and education. Over 30 states operate EBT systems and others are under consideration.

The basic idea is that recipients will either get electronic transfers to their bank account, or be able to download to their smart cards. The benefit is not only the reduction of the cost from 50 cents/per check, to 2 cents, but also the reduction of fraud. With biometrics coming to smart cards and PCs, officials expect fraud to be reduced substantially. For more information see **financenet.gov**.

Governments not only use EBT, but also smart cards as purchasing media for procurement. See Anonymous (1999) for details.

GOVERNMENT TO BUSINESS AND BUSINESS TO GOVERNMENT

Governments attempt to automate their interactions with business **(government to business, G2B)**. Two areas that receive a lot of attention are e-procurement and selling government surpluses.

E-procurement.

Governments buy large amounts of MROs and material direct from many suppliers. In many cases, a RFQ or tendering system is mandated by law. These requisitions were done manually for years; now they are moving online. In principle, the systems are basically *reverse auction* systems (buy-side systems). An example is briefly described in the Hong Kong system (the Update's Real World Case, ets.gove.hk). For information about such reverse auctions, see **buyers.gov**. Governments provide all the support for such tendering systems, as shown in Application Case 3.4.

E-auctions.

Governments auction surpluses ranging from vehicles to foreclosed real estate all over the world. Such auctions used to be done manually, then were moved to private networks, and now they are being moved online. Governments can use third-party auction sites such as eBay, **Bid4assets.com** or **freemarkets.com** for this purpose. The General Services Administration in the United States launched in January 2001, a property auction site online (**GSAAuctions.gov**), where real-time auctions for surpluses and seized goods are conducted. Some of these auctions are restricted to dealers; others are open to the public (see **Govexec.com**, January 18, 2001).

For an example of diversified applications in Switzerland see Schubert and Hausler (2001).

APPLICATION CASE 3.4

Contract Management in Australia

The development of contracting asset management solutions for the public sector in the online environment is the focus for the Western Australian (WA) government agency Contract and Management Services (CAMS). CAMS Online allows government agencies to search existing contracts to discover how to access the commonly used contracts across government, and assists suppliers wanting to sell to the government. Suppliers can view the current tenders on the Western Australia Government Contracting Information Bulletin Board, and download tender documents from this site.

CAMS Online provides government departments and agencies with unbiased, expert advice on e-commerce, the Internet, satellite services, and how-to's on building a bridge between the technological needs of the public sector and the expertise of the private sector. The center is divided into three sections—e-commerce, Internet services, and satellite services.

E-Commerce

Government Buying: Government clients can purchase goods and services on the CAMS Internet Marketplace—from sending a purchase order to receiving an invoice and paying for an item.

WA Government Electronic Market: This procurement market provides online supplier catalogs for common use contracts and other contract arrangements, electronic purchase orders and goods receipting electronic invoicing, EFT, and check and credit card payments.

ProcureLink: An established CAMS service that sends electronic purchase orders to suppliers for electronic data interchange (EDI), EDI Post, facsimile, and the Internet.

DataLink: Enables the transfer of data using a secure and controlled environment for message management. DataLink is an ideal solution for government agencies needing to exchange large volumes of operational information.

SalesNet: The government secures credit card payment solutions for the sale of government goods and services across the Internet.

Internet Services

ServiceNet: A government-controlled computer network that operates within a secure and firewall protected environment, offering Internet access in general and access to Procurelink, SalesNet, WA FastPay and Online buying through the WA Government Electronic Market using desktop browser technologies.

Satellite Services

Westlink: A service delivering adult training and educational programs to remote areas and schools, including rural and regional communities.

Video conferencing: This service offers two-way video and audio links enabling people to see and hear each other at up to eight sites at any one time. Access to the Online Services Center is via the CAMS Web site at **cams.wa.gov.au**.

G2E in the U.S. Navy

The U.S. Navy is using e-government techniques to improve the flow of information to sailors and their families. Because long shipboard deployments cause strains on navy families, the Navy in 1995 began seeking ways to ensure that quality-of-life information reaches navy personnel and their loved ones all over the world. Examples of quality-of-life information include self-help, deployment support, stress management, parenting advice, and relocation assistance.

Lifelines (lifelines2000.org) uses the Internet, simulcasting, cable television, satellite broadcasting, teleconfer-encing, dish TV, and the EchoStar system for overseas broadcasting. The Navy has found that certain media channels are more appropriate for certain types of information.

Lifelines regularly features live broadcasts, giving forward-deployed sailors and their families welcome information and, in some cases, a taste of home. On the Web, an average of 2,000 people access the Lifelines site each day.

The government provides several other services to Navy personnel. Notable are online banking, personal finance services, and insurance. Educational and training is also provided online.

GOVERNMENT TO GOVERNMENT

The **government-to-government (G2G)** category includes all intragovernmental activities, primarily among different government units, as well as nonbusiness dealings with other governments. Some examples of G2G in the United States include:

INTELINK. Intelink is an intranet that is based on classified networks which have created a new spirit of sharing information among the numerous intelligence agencies.

BUYERS.GOV OF THE GENERAL SERVICES ADMINISTRATION. This Web site (buyers.gov) is seeking to make the most out of newly developed Web-based procurement methods. Buyers.gov is an experiment in technologies such as demand aggregation and reverse auctions.

FEDERAL CASE REGISTRY (DEPARTMENT OF HEALTH AND HUMAN SERVICES). This service, which is available at acf.dhhs.gov/programs/cse/newhire/fcr/fcr.htm, helps state governments locate information about child support, including data on paternity and enforcement.

PROCUREMENT MARKETING AND ACCESS NETWORK (SMALL BUSINESS ADMINISTRATION). This service (http://pro-net.sba.gov) presents PRO-Net, a searchable database that contracting officers can use to find products and services sold by small, disadvantaged, and women-owned businesses.

For more examples, see this Update's Real World Case, and govexec/com/features/1100/egov/g2g.

GOVERNMENT TO EMPLOYEES

Governments employ large numbers of people. Therefore, governments provide e-services (G2E) to their employees in a manner similar to that of private organizations. One example is the Lifeline services provided by the U.S. government to Navy employees and their families (see Application Case 3.5).

3.9 Implementing E-government

As in any other organization, one can also find large numbers of EC applications in government organizations. And like any other organization, governments want to transform themselves to the digital era. This lengthy *transformation* is divided in a Deloitte and Touch's report (see Wong, 2000) into the following six stages, as shown in Figure 3.6.

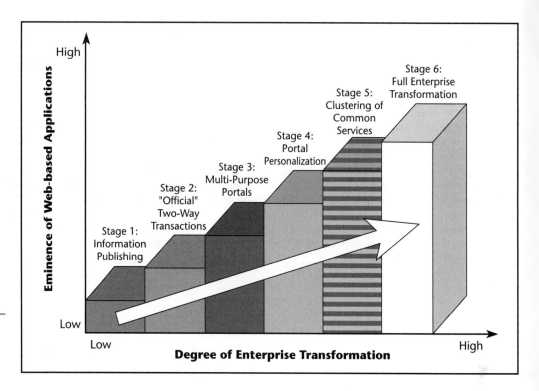

Figure 3.6

The Stages in
E-government

Source: Deloitte Research (see
Wong [2000]).

Here are the essentials of the six stages:

Stage 1: Information Publishing/Dissemination. Individual government departments set up their own Web sites that provide the public with information about them, the range of services available, and contacts for further assistance. At this stage, governments establish an electronic encyclopedia to reduce the number of phone calls customers need to make to reach the appropriate employee who can fulfill their service requests. Also, paperwork and help-line employee can be reduced.

Stage 2: "Official" Two-Way Transactions. With the help of legally valid digital signatures and secure Web sites, customers are able to submit personal information to—and conduct monetary transactions with—individual departments. At this stage, customers must be convinced of the department's ability to keep their information private and free from piracy. For example, the local government of Lewisham, United Kingdom, lets citizens claim income support and housing benefits using an electronic form. In Singapore, payment to citizen and from citizen to various government agencies can be performed online.

Stage 3: Multipurpose Portals. At this point, customer-centric governments make a big breakthrough in service delivery. Based on the fact that customer needs can cut across department boundaries, a portal allows customers to use a single point of entry to send and receive information and to process monetary transactions across multiple departments. For example, in addition to acting as a gateway to its agencies and related governments, the government of South Australia's portal (**sa.gov.au**) features a link for citizens to pay bills (utilities, automotive), manage bank accounts and conduct personal stock brokering (see Application Case 3.6).

Stage 4: Portal Personalization. Through stage 3, customers can access a variety of services at a single Web site. In stage 4, government puts even more power into customers' hands by allowing them to customize portals with their desired features. To accomplish this, governments will need much more sophisticated Web programming that allows interfaces to be user-manipulated. The added benefit of portal personalization is that governments will get a more accurate read on cus-

E-government in the state of Victoria, Australia

Titled Maxi, the e-government initiative went live online on December 9, 1997, with more than 30 government-related services available, including registering vehicles, obtaining driver licenses, ordering birth certificates, notifying the government about changes of address, and paying utilities bills and fines. Maxi.com.au is designed around the concept of "life events," similar to the Hong Kong initiative (see this Update's Real World Case). It embraces not only the government's relationship with the citizens and the business sector, but also the different tiers of the government.

The site provides services 24 hours a day, every day of the year. This project is part of the "Victorian Government's Vic 21 strategy" that aims to modernize government-to-citizen services.

The Internet portal features four service areas: (1) general information about Maxi, (2) bill payment and services by agencies, (3) life events (change of address, getting married, turning 18), and (4) a business channel. The business channel offers a range of services to help existing firms expand their practices and start up new businesses.

Maxi kiosks are located in shopping centers, libraries, government offices, and other public locations around Victoria. The fitting out includes a touch screen, bar code scanner, A4 printer, thermal receipt printer, and full EFTPOS (electronic funds transfer at point-of-sale) capability for paying with debit or credit cards. Maxi employs SecureNet Certificates to provide customers with digital certificates of authenticity and public keys for digital signatures.

To encourage better acceptance, Maxi offered a lucky draw to users from July 1 to December 31, 2000. Any one of Maxi usages entitled the users to participate in the lucky draw. The more transactions on Maxi, the better the chance for a citizen to become a winner.

Customer adoption of Maxi has exceeded the government's expectations. One year after Maxi first went live, more than 24,000 transactions were conducted monthly over the network, tripling the initial target of 8,000 a month. Maxi has also given citizens new levels of convenience, with 40 percent of all transactions occurring outside normal 9-to-5 business hours.

---

tomer preference for electronic versus non-electronic service options. Like in industry, this will allow for a true CRM in government. In March 2001, such a portal was in planning stages in several state and country governments.

Stage 5: Clustering of Common Services. Stage 5 is where real transformation of government structure takes shape. As customers now view once-disparate services as a unified package through the portal, their perception of departments as distinct entities will begin to blur. They will recognize groups of transactions rather than groups of agencies. To make it happen, governments will cluster services along common lines to accelerate the delivery of shared services. In other words, a business restructuring will take place.

Stage 6: Full Integration and Enterprise Transformation. What started as a digital encyclopedia is now a full-service center, personalized to each customer's needs and preferences. At this stage, old walls defining silos of services have been torn down, and technology is integrated across the new government structure to bridge the shortened gap between the front and back offices. In some countries, new departments will have formed from the remains of predecessors. Others will have the same names, but their interiors will look nothing like they did before e-government.

TRANSFORMATION

The speed at which a government moves from stage 1 toward stage 6 varies, but usually it is very slow. Some of the determining factors are the degree of resistance to change by government employees, the adoption rate of applications by citizens, the available budget, and the legal environment. Deloitte Research found that in 2000, most governments were still in stage 1. They propose an eight-point plan to expedite the transformation progress:

- Define a vision—and a v-business case—for e-government.
- Build customer trust with privacy, security and confidentiality.
- Plan technology for growth and customer-friendliness.

- Manage access channels to optimize value.
- Weigh insourcing versus outsourcing.
- Establish investment plans that work without funding cycles.
- Understand the impact of fees for transactions.
- Include a strong change management program.

Implementating G2B.

Implementation of G2B is easier. In some countries, such as Hong Kong, the implementation is outsourced to a private company who pays all the expenses in exchange for getting transaction fees at a later time.

SECURITY ISSUES

Governments are concerned about maintaining the security and privacy of citizens' data. One area is that of health care. From a medical point of view, it is necessary to have quick access to people's data, and the Internet and smart cards provide such capabilities; however, the protection of such data is very expensive. Many local and central governments are working on this topic.

DEVELOPING PORTALS

Many vendors offer tools for building government and corporate portals, as well as hosting services. Representative vendors are **tibco.com** (Portal Builder), Computer Associates at **ca.com** (Jasmine ii Portal), and **Plumtree.com**.

NON-INTERNET E-GOVERNMENT

Today, e-government is associated with the Internet. However, governments have been using other networks, especially internally, to improve the governments' operations for over 15 years. For example, on January 17, 1994, there was a major earthquake in Southern California. About 114,000 buildings were damaged and more than 500,00 victims turned to the Federal Emergency Management Agency for help. Initially, tired and dazed citizens stood hours in line to register and have in-person interviews. An e-government application was installed to expedite the process of issuing checks to citizens. Citizens called an 800 number and the operators entered the information collected directly into online electronic forms. Then the data traveled electronically to the mobile disaster inspectors. Once checked, data went electronically to financial management and finally to check issuing. The data never touched a paper, and the cycle time has been reduced by more than 50 percent. Non-Internet e-government initiatives will probably be converted sooner or later to Internet-based ones.

3.10 Customer-to-Customer and Peer-to-Peer Applications

CUSTOMER-TO-CUSTOMER E-COMMERCE

Auctions are an example of **customer-to-customer (C2C)** e-commerce. Millions of individuals are buying and selling on eBay and hundreds of other Web sites worldwide. In addition to auctions, C2C activities include the following.

Classified Ads.

People sell to people by using classified ads. Internet-based classified ads have several advantages over newspaper classified ads.

- Ads include national, rather than local selection. This greatly increases the supply. For example, **classifieds2000.com** contains a list of about 500,000 cars.
- A search engine helps to narrow the search.
- Photos are available in many cases.
- Ads are free for private parties.

- Ads can be edited easily.
- Placing an ad in one Web site (e.g. classifieds2000.com) brings it automatically into the classified sections of numerous partners. This increases the exposure, with no cost.
- Special features that expedite search are available on some sites. Free personalized services are available.

The major categories of classified ads are similar to those found in the newspaper, including vehicles, real estate, employment, general merchandise, collectibles, computers, pets, tickets, and travel. Classified ads are available in most ISPs (AOL, etc.), in some search engines (Excite, etc.), telephone companies, Internet directories, newspapers, and more. Once users find an ad and can get the details,they can e-mail or call the other party.

Personal Services.

Numerous personal services are available on the Internet. Some are in the classified ads, but others are in specialized Web sites and directories.

C2C Barter Exchanges.

Several exchanges for consumer-to-consumer bartering are available (e.g., swapvillage.com). For a complete list, see ecompany.com.

Consumer Exchanges.

Many exchanges are available for transactions between individuals. A list of exchanges by category is available at ecompany.com.

PEER-TO-PEER NETWORKS AND APPLICATIONS

Peer-to-peer (P2P) computer architecture is a type of network in which each workstation (or PC) has similar capabilities. This is in contrast with client-server architecture in which some computers serve other computers. As peers, the computers share data, processing, and devices with each other. In P2P the computers communicate directly with each other, rather than through a central server.

The main benefit of P2P is that it can enormously expand the universe of information accessible from a personal computer—users are not confined to just Web pages. Additionally, some proponents claim that a well-designed P2P system can offer better security, reliability, and availability of content than the client-server model, on which the Web is based. The acronym P2P also stands for People-to-People, Person-to-Person, and Point-to-Point.

Characteristics of P2P Systems.

Peer-to-peer systems involve the following seven key characteristics:

- User interfaces load outside of a Web browser.
- User computers can act as both clients and servers.
- The overall system is easy to use and is well integrated.
- The system includes tools to support users wanting to create content or add functionality.
- The system provides connections with other users.
- The system does something new or exciting.
- The system supports "cross-networking" protocols such as SOAP or XML-RPC.

The characteristics of P2P computing show that devices can join the network from anywhere with little effort. Instead of dedicated LANs, the Internet itself becomes the network of choice. Easier configuration and control over the applications allows people without network savvy to join the user community. In fact, P2P signifies a shift in emphasis in peer networking from the hardware to the applications.

Peer-to-peer networking is connecting people *directly* to other people. It provides an easy setup system for sharing, publishing, and interacting that requires no system

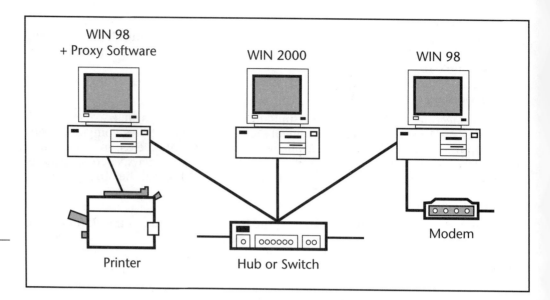

Figure 3.7

Peer-to-Peer Networks

Each resource can be shared by all.

administration knowledge. The system wraps everything up into a user-friendly interface and lets people share or communicate with each other.

An example of P2P network is graphically illustrated in Figure 3.7. The workstations shown in the graph perform a computer-to-computer communication via their operating systems.

P2P APPLICATIONS IN C2C

Napster—The File-Sharing Utility.

Napster is an example of C2C, where people can enter files of other people, to share music and games by logging into the Napster system. The network also allows users to search other members' hard drives for a particular file, including data files created by users or copied from elsewhere. Napster had more than 20 million members by the end of 2000.

The Napster server functions as a directory, which indicates the list of files being shared by other users. Once logged in to the server, users can search the songs they like and locate the file owner. They can directly access the owner's computer and download the songs they have chosen. Napster also includes chat rooms to connect its millions of users.

Other Providers

An even purer version of P2P is Gnutella, a P2P program that dispenses with the central database altogether. For games, try **zone.com** (from Microsoft), **heat.net**, and **battle.net**. As a matter of fact, ICQ (the instant messenger-type chat room) can be considered a hybrid P2P technology.

COMMERCIAL APPLICATIONS IN BUSINESS C2C.

With P2P, users can sell digital goods directly from their computers rather than going through centralized servers. If users want to sell on eBay, they are required to put an item on eBay's site and upload a photo. If an auction site uses file sharing, it can direct customers to the PC seller where buyers can find plenty of information, photos, and even videos about the items being sold.

Computer Resources and Data File Sharing.

Sharing of disk drives and printers across the network is quite common in modern office settings. Moreover, data files or other types of information sharing in the local area network (LAN), and the sharing of program files between the computers through Windows NT, actually can be regarded as a type of P2P networking.

Intrabusiness Applications.

Several companies are using P2P to facilitate internal collaboration. For example, in 1990, Intel wrote a file transfer program called NetBatch, which allows chip designers to utilize the additional processing power of colleagues' computers across sites in California, Arizona, and even foreign countries such as Israel. Intel saved more than $500 million during 1991–2000.

BUSINESS-TO-BUSINESS.

P2P could be a technology panacea for system innovators building B2B exchanges. The reason is that Lotus Notes and other business-process automation packages are cumbersome. With P2P people can share information, but they are not required to send it to an unknown server. Because of a lack of trust in corporate boundaries with exchanges, companies can keep documents in-house instead of on an unknown server.

Several companies are using the P2P architecture as a base for speeding up business transactions. The following are some examples:

- Hilgraeve of Monroe, Michigan, has a technology called DropChute that establishes a point-to-point connection between two computers and allows users to transfer files. The company has won a U.S. patent for its P2P communication process and touts four levels of encryption and virus-scanning protection.
- Fort Knox Escrow Service, Atlanta, leverages DropChute to enable clients to deliver material electronically. "Instead of having to wait for an overnight package, we can do it all over the Internet," says Jeanna Israel, Fort Knox's director of operations.
- Certapay.com is a P2P e-mail payment platform that enables e-banking customers to send and receive money using only an e-mail address.

According to worldstreet.com, the real winners within the B2B segment will be companies that deliver rich, extensible, balanced, two-way collaborative interactions that are:

- dynamic (supporting extensible, interactive communications between people, applications, systems and devices),
- real-time, (providing delivery of rich, personalized, on-demand information),
- collaborative (delivering a venue for secure interactions between any number of participants, some of whom could not previously find each other),
- structured (spoken in an industry-specific dialect that facilitates communication and transactions),
- relevant (focused on the participants' topics of interest at that time),
- service-based (integrating existing workflows, systems, devices, and applications to provide an optimum method for determining what information is exchanged and how it is delivered),
- cost effective (reducing the costs of establishing and maintaining online business relationships),
- client-focused (enabling the exchange of new kinds of information—or previously inaccessible information—and delivering the highest quality, and most personalized service possible).

Peer networks effectively address the Web's B2B deficiencies. The model is a natural fit for the needs of business, since business relationships are intrinsically peer to peer. Peer networks allow businesses to communicate, interact, and transact with each other as never before by making the business relationships interactive, dynamic, real-time, and balanced—within and between enterprises.

The success of P2P in B2B is not clear. It depends in part on the ability of the technology to address security and scalability issues. For further discussion see McAfee (2000).

Business–to–Consumer.

There are several potential applications in marketing and advertisement. For example, isdigital.com is combining P2P with collaborative filtering. Its product will work as follows. Assume a user conducts a search for a product:

Step 1: A user enters a search keyword.

Step 2: The keyword is sent to 100 peers, which search local indices of the Web pages they have visited.

Step 3: Those computers also relay the query to 100 of their peers, and that group submits it to 100 of theirs, yielding, in theory, up to one million computers queried.

Step 4: The resulting URLs are returned to the user, weighted in favor of most recently visited pages and peers with similar interests.

3.11   Managerial Issues

The following are several issues that need to be dealt with by management.

1. **Intranet Content Management.** The content delivered on an intranet is created by many individuals. Two potential risks exist. First, corporate proprietary information may not be protected enough, so, unauthorized people may have access to it. Second, appropriate intranet Netiquettes must be maintained, otherwise, unethical or even illegal behavior may develop. Therefore, managing the intranet content is a must, including its frequent updates.

2. **Designing Corporate Portals.** Corporate portals are the gateways to the corporate information and knowledge. Appropriate portal design is a must not only for easy and efficient navigation, but also for recognizing that portals portray the corporate image to employees and to business partners who are allowed access to it. This issue is related to content management.

3. **Selling the Intranet.** In some companies there is a problem of selling the intranet. If paper documents are replaced, then employees must check the intranet frequently. Depending on the organizational culture, in many cases employees often are not using intranets to their fullest capacity. Some companies are making formal presentations to employees including online and offline training. Others provide incentives to users; some penalize nonusers. One approach is the creation of an Intranet Day (see *Internetweek*, May 3, 1999, p. 27).

4. **Accessing the Intranet from the Outside.** The more applications a company places on the intranet, the more important the need to allow employees to access it while they are outside the organization. This may create security problems, especially when employees try to do it via a modem.

5. **Connectivity.** Intranets need to be connected to the Internet and in many cases to extranets for B2B applications. Because many partners may be involved and several communication and network protocols, careful planning is needed.

6. **Finding Intranet Applications.** The intranet technology is mature enough and its applications are fairly standard. Look at vendors' case studies for ideas as well as intranetjournal.com/casestudies and google.com (intranet case studies). Another place to investigate is cio.com/forums/intranet/cases.html.

7. **Your Organization and E-government.** If your organization is doing business with the government, eventually you will do it online. You may find new online business opportunities with the government, because governments are getting serious about going online. Some even mandate it as the only way to conduct B2G and G2B.

8. **P2P Applications.** Watch for new developments of tools and applications. Some experts say a major revolution is coming for faster and cheaper online communication and collaboration. As with any other new innovation, it will take time to mature.

Summary

The completion of this Update helps in attaining the following learning objectives:

- **Defining intrabusiness EC.** Intrabusiness EC refers to all EC initiatives conducted within one organization. These can be activities between an organization and its employees, between SBUs in the organization, and among the organization's employees.
- **The intranet and its use in organizations.** The intranet is the corporate internal network that is constructed with Internet protocols and tools, such as search engines and browsers. It is used for internal communication, collaboration, and discovery of information in various internal databases. It is protected by firewalls against unauthorized access.
- **The relationship between the corporate portal and the intranet.** The corporate portal is the gateway through which users access the various applications conducted over the intranet, such as training, accessing databases or receiving customized news.
- **E-government to citizens.** Governments worldwide are providing a large variety of services to citizens over the Internet. Such initiatives increase citizens' satisfaction (more responsive government, less waiting time) and decreases government expenses in providing customer service applications.
- **Other E-government activities.** Governments, like any other organizations can use EC applications for great savings. Notable are e-procurement using reverse auctions, payments to and from citizens and businesses, auction of surpluses, and using electronic travel and expense management systems.
- **Applications of peer-to-peer technology.** Peer-to-peer technology allows direct communication for sharing files and for collaboration. While Napster gets a lot of publicity for its support of music and game sharing among millions of its members, the same technology is used in both B2B and in intrabusiness.

Key Terms

Business-to-employees (B2E)	Government-to-business (G2B)
C-commerce	Government-to-government (G2G)
Corporate portal	Internet portal
Customer-to-Customer (C2C)	Intrabusiness EC
E-government	Intranet
Enterprise portal	Knowledge curve intranet
Government-to-citizens (G2C)	Peer-to-peer (P2P) technology

Questions for Review

1. Define intrabusiness and list its major categories.
2. Define corporate portal.
3. Define an intranet.
4. Describe peer-to-peer technology.
5. List the major types of e-government.
6. List the major types of portals.
7. List the major content components of a portal.
8. What is included in G2C?
9. What is B2E? Provide an example.
10. Define C2C and provide an example.

Questions for Discussion

1. Discuss the relationship between corporate portal and the intranets.
2. Compare and contrast Internet portals (such as Yahoo!) and corporate portals.
3. Which e-government EC activities are intrabusiness? Why?
4. Discuss the relationship between a knowledge management and a portal.
5. Discuss some of the potential ethical and legal implications of people using P2P to download music, games, and so forth.
6. The interest in intranets is coming back. Discuss the reasons why.
7. Identify the benefits of G2C to citizens and to governments.
8. Discuss the relationship between B2E and portals.
9. Some say that B2G is just B2B. Discuss.
10. Discuss the major properties of P2P.

Exercises

1. Concerning Amway Inc. (Section 3.1):
   a. Describe how the information access problems affected the R&D department in developing new products.
   b. Describe the role of the business intelligence and knowledge portal in R&D at Amway.
   c. Enter amway.com and examine its corporate structure. What kind of groupware can help the salespeople?
   d. Find a couple of business intelligence and knowledge management portals and compare those with Artemis.
2. Concerning the Cadence Design Systems, Inc. example (Section 3.6):
   a. What was the purpose of adopting an intranet for Cadence?
   b. What are the functions available in the OnTrack system?
   c. What are the benefits realized by adopting OnTrack?
   d. Describe the outsourcing strategy of Cadence.
   e. Describe the training requirement for OnTrack.

Internet Exercises

1. Enter whitehouse.gov/government/index and review the "Gateway to Government." Rate it on the Delloitte Research scale (what stage?). Review the available tours. Make suggestions for the government to improve this portal.
2. Read the issue paper, "E-mail communication between government and citizens," at rand.org/publications/IP/IP178. What are the major conclusions and recommendations of this study?
3. Enter oece.org/Puma/citizens and identify the studies conducted by the organization for Economic Operation and Development (OECD) in Europe on the topic of e-government. What are the major concerns?
4. Enter fcw.com and read the latest news on e-government. Identify initiatives not covered in this Update. Check the B2G corner.
5. Enter ca.com/products and register. Then take the jasmineii_portal/test_drive. (Flash Player from Macromedia is required.)
6. Enter xdegrees.com, centrata.com, and Pointera.com and evaluate some of the solutions offered. How can they expedite a search for a song at gnutella.co.uk? Also, enter Aberdeen.com to learn more about P2P applications.
7. Enter knowledgespace.com. This knowledge base resides on Andersen's intranet. Sign up for the service (if still available free for a trial period). Why is such a system better when utilized on the intranet? Why not use a CD-ROM-based technology?

8. Enter govxec.com/egov and explore the latest developments in G2C, G2B (and B2G) and G2G.
9. Enter worldstreet.com and go to "products." Identify all potential B2B applications, and prepare a report about them.
10. Enter procurement.com and govexec.com and identify recent e-procurement initiatives and summarize their unique aspects.
11. Enter IQ Magazine at Cisco.com and find information about employee portals and P2P/B2B. Prepare a report about them.

Team Exercises and Role Playing

1. Enter oecd.org/puma/citizens and examine available country reports. Also, use google.com and govexec.com/features, to find information about G2C. Compare initiatives in several countries and identify ways to strengthen government-citizen connections. Write a report.
2. Create four teams each representing one of the following: G2C, G2B, G2E and G2G. Each team prepares a plan of its major activities in a small country such as Denmark, Finland, or Singapore. Then, a fifth team deals with the coordination and collaboration of all e-government activities in each country.

REAL WORLD CASE: *E-government Initiatives in Hong Kong*

The Hong Kong SAR government, China (HK), initiated several e-government projects under the Digital 21 IT strategy (info.gov.hk/digital21). The major projects described here are

- the electronic service delivery scheme (EDS),
- the interactive government services directory (IGSD),
- the electronic tendering system (ETS),
- the HKSAR Government Information Center, and
- the HK post office certification service (Post e-Cert).

The highlights of these initiatives are provided here. Further information can be found in the specific URLs presented at info.gov.hk, for each specific program.

The Electronic Service Delivery Scheme (ESD).

This project provides a major infrastructure through which the public can transact business electronically with 38 different public services provided by 11 government agencies. Examples are:

1. **Transport Department:** Applications for driving and vehicle licenses, appointments for vehicle examinitions and road tests, reporting change of address, and so forth.
2. **Immigration:** Application for birth/death/marriage certificates, making appointment for ID card issuance, application for foreign domestic helpers, communication on any other issue concerning immigration.
3. **HK Tourist Association:** Tourist information, maps, answers to queries.

4. **Labour Department:** Register job openings, search for jobs, search for applicants, FAQs regarding legal issues, employee's compensation plans, and so forth.
5. **Social Welfare Department:** Applications for senior citizen cards and card-scheme participation, welfare information, registration for volunteer scheme, request for charitable fund-raising permits, and so forth.
6. **Inland Revenue Department (Taxation):** Filing tax returns electronically, electronic payment program, change of address, interactive tax Q&A, applications for sole proprietor certificate, application for business registrations, purchase tax reserve certificates, and so forth.
7. **Registration and Electoral Office:** Application for voter registration, change of address, interactive Q&A.
8. **Trade and Industry Department:** Business license information and application, SME information center online.
9. **Treasury Department:** Electronic bill payment.
10. **Rating and Valuation Department:** Changes of rates and/or government rent payers' particulars, interactive Q&A.
11. **Innovation and Technology Commission:** Information on technology funding schemes. Electronic application for funding.

These services are provided in Chinese and English under the ESD life title. The project is managed by ESD Services Limited (esdlife.com). For additional information, see esd.gov.hk/esdlife.

In addition to these services, the Web site includes eight ESD clubs or communities. The public can sign up for a club, get information, share experiences, or just chat. The eight clubs are: ESDbaby (for new parents, family planning, etc); ESDkids (how to raise kids); ESDteens (a meeting point for the teens on music, culture, learning, etc); ESD1822 (lifestyle, education, jobs, etc., for 18 to 22 year olds); EDScouples (information on getting married and building a family); ESDprime (jobs, education, entertainment, investment, travel, etc, for adults); ESDsenior (health care, fitness, education, lifestyle); and ESDhospice (complete services for the end of life).

The Interactive Government Services Directory

The interactive government services directory (IGSD) is an interactive service that enables the public to get public information and services not included in the ESD. For example, it includes:

- Telephone and Web site directory of public services with information and links to hundreds of services.
- Interactive investment guide of industry department (investing in Hong Kong)
- Interactive employment services
- Interactive road traffic information

The Electronic Tendering System (ETS)

The electronic tendering system (ETS) is a G2B Web site that manages the reverse auctions conducted by the government supplies department. It includes supplier registration, notification of tenders, downloading of tendering documents, interactive Q&A, submission of tender offers and more. The HKSAR government conducts more than 5,000 tenders a year. For further information, see ets.com.hk.

The HKSAR Government Information Center

It is the official government Web site (info.gov.hk), which enables the public to obtain news, government notices, guides to major government services, leisure and cultural activities, and more.

The HK Post E-cert

This site is the home for the Hong Kong public certification authority (hongkongpost.com). The Hong Kong Post created a PKI system, which issues digital certificates (Post E-cert) to individuals and to organizations. It also maintains a certificate respository and directory of all certificates issued, so that the public can verify the validity of the certificates. The Post E-cert also issues certificates to servers and to security systems.

Note: Accessibility to the e-government portal is available not only from PCs, but also from hundreds of kiosks placed in many public places in Hong Kong.

Questions

1. Which of the five initiatives is a G2C, G2B, C2G, and G2E?
2. Visit info.gov.hk/digital21 and identify the goals of the e-government initiatives.
3. How will the role of the HKSAR government change when the initiatives are matured and fully utilized?
4. Enter esdlife.com and compare the services with those offered in Singapore (ecitizen.gov.sg). What are the major differences? Also see tnbt.com, Dec. 8, 2000, News.
5. View Figure 3.5. What applications could be added in the future by the HKSAR government?

References and Bibliography

A. Aneja et al. 2000. "Corporate Portal Framework for Transforming Content Chaos on Intranets." Intel Technology Journal, Q1.

Anonymous. 1999. "The Feds Play Their Card Hands," Credit Card Management, January.

Anonymous. 2000. "Experts Offer 5 Keys to Successful Portals" F/S Analyzer Case Studies, February.

K. Bacon et al. 2001. E-Government: The Blue Print. New York: John Wiley & Sons.

R. Bernard. 1997. The Corporate Intranet. New York: John Wiley & Sons.

J. Bort and B. Felix. 1997. Building an Extranet: Connect Your Intranet with Vendors and Customers. New York: John Wiley & Sons.

J. Cashin. 1998. Intranet Strategies and Technologies for Building Effective Enterprisewide Intranet Systems. Charleston, South Carolina: Computer Technology Research Corp.

D. Chaffee. 1998. Groupware, Workflow and Intranets: Reengineering the Enterprise with Collaborative Software. Boston: Digital Press.

S. Y. Choi. and Whinston, A.B. 2000. The Internet Economy: Technology and Practice, Austin, Texas: SmartEcon Publishing.

K. Damore and M. Savage. 2000. "Peer-to-Peer Pressure." Computer Reseller News, 28 August.

J. S. Gonzalez. 1998. The 21st Century Intranet. Upper Saddle River, New Jersey: Prentice Hall.

S. Grisworld. 1997. Corporate Intranet Development. Rocklin, CA: Prima Publishing.

B. Hopkins. 1997. How to Design and Post Information on a Corporate Intranet. Hampshire, United Kingdom: Gower Pub. Co.

T. Kounadis. 2000. "How to Pick the Best Portal." e-Business Advisor, August.

T. M. Koulopoulos. 1999. "Corporate Portals: Make Knowledge Accessible to All." InformationWeek, 26 April.

A. Laalo. 1998"Intranets and Competitive Intelligence: Creating Access to Knowledge," Competitive Intelligence Review, Vol. 9, no. 4.

T. Lister.1999. "Ten Commandments for Converting Your Intranet into a Secure Extranet." UNIX Review's Performance Computing, July.

A. McAff, (2000, November-December), "The Napsterization of B2B," Harvard Business Review.

M. Miller et al. 1998. Managing the Corporate Intranet. New York: John Wiley & Sons.

N. Palmer. 2000. "Transform Your Business into a B2B Portal." e-Business Advisor, April.

A. Richardson. 1997. The Intranet: Opportunities within the Corporate Environment. Elsevier Science Online.

B. Robinson, 2000,. "Shopping for the Right B2G Model." Federal Computer Week, 28 August.

P. Schubert and U. Hausler, (2000, Jan.), "E-Government Meets E-Business: A portal site for startup Companies in Switzerland," proceedings, HICSS, Hawaii.

J. Schwartz. 2000. "E voting: Its Day Has Not Come Just Yet," New York Times, 27 November.

Special Report. 2000. E-Government: The Next American Revolution. The Hart-Teeter study on e-government at excelgov.org/egopoll.

S. Stellin. 2000. "Intranets Nurture Companies From the Inside." New York Times, 29 January.

D. Tapscott. 2000. Digital Capital: Harnessing the Power of Business Webs. Boston: Harvard Business School Press.

R. L. Wagner and E. Englemann. 1997. Building and Managing the Corporate Intranet. New York: McGraw-Hill.

J. Watson and J. Fenner. 2000. "Understanding Portals." Information Management Journal, July.

W. Y. Wong. 2000. At the Dawn of E-government. New York: Deloitte Research, Deloitte & Touche.